YOUR DREAM JOB

How to Land the Job of Your Dreams

Foolproof Interview Skills

JO BANKS

i

Published by What Next? Media – sales@whatnextconsultancy.co.uk

For Justine...

Thanks for being there!

"The best way to predict the future is to create it."

(Abraham Lincoln)

Contents

FOREWORD

"Passion is the difference between having a job and a career."

Welcome to Book 4 in the *'Your Dream Job'* series. This programme has been designed specifically to give you all the tools, techniques and support you need to land Your Dream Job. It covers everything from successfully managing job loss, getting clear about your next role, effective CV writing and, foolproof interview skills, to how to handle the all-important job offer and everything else in between.

Following from the success of my second book, *'Land Your Dream Job Now!'* I received feedback suggesting that it would be useful for readers to be able to purchase individual sections, specific to their needs, e.g. CV Writing, Interview Skills, etc. Thereby, making it more cost effective.

With that in mind, I have taken the original 'Dream Job' book and broken it down into individual sections, each addressing a particular topic within the job search process. This has allowed me the opportunity to revise the original content and add additional information that didn't make the original edit.

HOW AM I QUALIFIED TO WRITE THIS BOOK?

I set up my own business, What Next Consultancy (UK) Ltd in 2009. Since then I've personally coached over 1,500 people with over 4,500 having attended 'What Next' Career Management Workshops. I personally work with clients to provide them with the tools, techniques and mindset adjustments necessary to identify what exactly it is they want, how/where to find it and how to go about getting it. Whether that entails a sideways move, promotion, or change of career, I help pave the way. I'm also proud to say that I've helped an ever-increasing number of clients start their own businesses.

Before setting up What Next, my background was in senior human resource management (HR), with a career spanning almost 20 years. During that time, I interviewed thousands of candidates ranging from forklift truck drivers to senior executives and CEOs. Having such an extensive background in recruitment enables me to instinctively know what companies are looking for during the selection process. It allows me to help my clients maximise their self-promotion, providing them with top tips that will put them ahead of their competitors, enabling them to land their dream job. It's often the small things that make a big difference.

OUTPLACEMENT & REDEPLOYMENT

At What Next, outplacement and redeployment programmes form part of our core offering. We provide both off-the-shelf and bespoke career management training to private and public sector organisations in the course of their ongoing commitment to their employees during change programmes, i.e. company restructures.

These courses include CV writing, interview skills, job hunting, presentation skills, together with how to start a business. We also offer one to one career management coaching sessions for more senior managers or those employees who are finding the transition particularly difficult.

ONE-TO-ONE SESSIONS

Depending on the organisation's budget and the individual's needs, a dedicated coach will work closely with the job seeker on a one-to-one basis covering the following areas:

- Assisting them in getting clear about exactly the type of job they want, the kind of company they want to work for, the industry, role content and remuneration, etc.
- Recognising their transferable skills.
- Producing an outstanding, achievement-based CV – which can be written by the coach (depending on budget).
- Devising a bespoke step-by-step job search project plan.
- Identifying and contacting prospective employers on the client's behalf.
- Bespoke interview preparation, explicitly tailored to individual roles.
- Researching the interviewing company, providing the client with a full report containing pertinent information for use in the interview.
- Reviewing the interview feedback.
- Helping manage negative emotions, e.g. interview nerves etc., as well as maintaining motivation at optimum levels.
- Managing the job offer process including negotiating the remuneration package.

- Acting as a general sounding board as well as providing motivation.
- Support during the first 90 days in post.

We offer a comprehensive service, and although we do employ underlying principles, we tailor our programmes directly to the needs of our clients. Having that flexibility allows us to provide practical guidance that gets results.

We continually review our content using feedback from our delegates, clients, and associates; we also incorporate key trends and advice gained from our extensive contacts within the recruitment industry. These include close links with recruitment consultants, internal recruiters, professional recruitment assessors and HR professionals. This feedback enables us to remain up-to-date, reflecting the current recruitment landscape.

It's that information and knowledge that I've included in this book. It contains the very best, up-to-date information available... I can, therefore, say with authority that **this stuff works!**

FREEBIES

As an additional 'thank you' for purchasing this book, there are free resources available, designed to complement the learning described in this programme.

Visit **yourdreamjob.co.uk** and sign up with a quality email address to receive regular updates and an assortment of useful tools and information designed specifically to help *you land 'Your Dream Job'.*

Signing up will ensure that you are added to our exclusive group of like-minded individuals, who wish to learn the top tips and techniques to enhance their job search and get the edge over their competitors. Head over to the website and sign up now!

yourdreamjob.co.uk

There is also a dedicated Facebook group which you are welcome to join:

facebook.com/YDJYourDreamJob/

INTRODUCTION

"If it doesn't challenge you, it won't change you."

WHY SHOULD YOU USE THIS PROGRAMME?

Since the last recession which started in 2008/2009, the face of recruitment has changed significantly. Recruiters had to rethink their strategies to find low-cost options that would deliver quality candidates. As a result, the recruitment industry had to react quickly in response to the changing needs of its clients.

This programme includes practical, simple, down to earth advice that if followed step by step, will give you all the tools you need to gain a competitive advantage in a post-recession world. This information has been proven to work consistently with thousands of job hunters. It is practically foolproof when applied as described.

The information I've included in this programme works, no matter what level you work at, what job you're looking for or whether you're currently in or out of work; the principles and activities are the same.

It is intentionally written in a simple, uncomplicated language with a common-sense approach that you'll find it easy to follow and implement.

The 'Your Dream Job' Programme

Within the 'Your Dream Job' programme, there are five individual books covering everything you need to know to land Your Dream Job. Following is a summary of each book and what it contains:

Book 1 – Managing Job Loss

- Facing Redundancy/Job Loss
- Managing Your Thoughts and Emotions
- Understanding the Change Curve
- Top Tips
- Taking Positive Action
- Frequently Asked Questions

Book 2 – Finding Your Dream Job

- Get Clear – Establish What You Want/Don't Want from Your Next Role

- Resigning from Your Current Employer
- What to Do If You Get a Counter Offer
- What to Do If a Job Offer Gets Retracted
- Know Your Rights
- What to Do If You Change Your Mind
- Frequently Asked Questions

WHAT YOU WILL LEARN IN THIS BOOK

Book 4 in the 'Dream Job' series, covers the following topics:

- ASSESSMENT TYPES & PREPARATION – As increasing numbers of high-calibre candidates continue to enter the job arena, with fewer and fewer roles available, recruitment processes have become more sophisticated. Recruiters now use a far broader range of assessment tools than ever before to pre-sift applications as cheaply as possible while ensuring that only the best candidates get through to costly face to face interviews.

  Preparation is essential when it comes to most recruitment assessments; did you know that **you can prepare for up to 85% of what will be asked in an interview?**

In this section, I'll describe the most typical selection methods, what to expect from them (how they work) and how to prepare to give you the best chance of success.

- INTERVIEW SKILLS – This chapter is packed full of top tips ranging from what to take into an interview, through to what to wear/how to present yourself. It also includes how to communicate and influence effectively to get yourself heard.

- PRESENTATION SKILLS – In this chapter, I explain a simple six-step, fool-proof process for planning and delivering an effective presentation. I've also included a section on how to prepare for an answer awkward question.

SUMMARY

I have helped thousands of people find the right job using the tools, techniques, hints and tips provided in the full Your Dream Job programme. To get the best results, I recommend using all the steps exactly as described.

Don't shy away from activities because they seem too hard, especially if they make you feel uncomfortable. Typically, they will be where you *should* be placing your focus. I also recommend creating a structured plan that you stick to and regularly review, ticking items off as you complete them. By doing this, you're more likely to achieve results, ultimately landing Your Dream Job.

NOTE - You will notice that I often repeat certain phrases or ideas throughout the programme. I make no apologies for this, as I consider these things to be critical aspects of job hunting, and, after all, repetition is the mother of skill!

Chapter 1 – Assessment Types & Preparation

"Fail to prepare, prepare to fail."

(Benjamin Franklin)

Overview Of Assessment Types

Companies are now using a more extensive range of recruitment assessment tools than ever before. Interviews used to be the primary or sole means of selection for many companies, and still remain the most widely utilised. However, as competition becomes increasingly fierce and the marketplace continues to have more high-calibre candidates than vacancies, many employers are turning to increasingly sophisticated methods to select the very best candidates in the most cost-effective ways.

As part of my research for this book, I interviewed freelance assessors who provide recruitment resource and expertise to corporations, primarily working on large recruitment projects, including graduate recruitment programmes. Therefore, the advice given here not only comes from my expert knowledge of assessment tools but directly from those who are currently involved in devising, managing and marking them.

Companies tend to use freelance assessors to support a range of evaluation activities such as video interviews, telephone interviews, assessment centres, etc. The benefit of using external people is that they are impartial and mark answers according to strict guidelines, eliminating the chance of any potential bias. It's also cost effective to bring in additional, expert resource rather than employing permanent headcount to cover ad hoc projects.

The following list is a compilation of the most popular selection methods which I cover in this book:

- Personal statements
- Online testing
- Video assessment
- Interviews:
  - Telephone
  - Skype/ Bluejeans
  - CV based
  - Competency-based

- Assessment Centres
- Covering letters
- Application forms
- Presentations

THE POWER OF PREPARATION

The quote I used at the beginning of the chapter, *"Fail to prepare, prepare to fail"* sums this chapter up nicely. One of the main reasons why candidates fail assessments, especially interviews and presentations, is a lack of preparation. Excessive candidate nerves can mainly be attributed to a lack of preparation. Candidates who do everything possible to prepare, usually find that their nerves, stress, and anxiety are automatically reduced as a result.

The purpose of any assessment (including interviews) is to determine how your skills and experience match those required for the job – as well as general personal 'fit' for the role and the company. With this in mind, **you can prepare for 80-85% of any interview**. Knowing this statistic, it never ceases to amaze me why so many people don't! Most candidates will research the company but fail to adequately prepare for questions around their own achievements and career history, nor do they design any intelligent questions to ask the interviewer.

When my clients go for an interview, I ask them to call me afterwards so that we can review their performance and understand any development areas. If they say, *"That went really badly"* my first question is always, *"Did you do all your preparation as we discussed?"* Often, the answer is, *"No"* and we work together to plan for what they need to do differently next time. For those who did do their preparation, I'll ask, *"Could you have done any more?"* Again, usually, the answer is, *"No"*. If that's the case, then the role or company just wasn't right for them, and they need to move onwards and upwards. Usually, something bigger and better will come along soon afterwards.

In summary, those who prepare thoroughly for interviews perform far better than those who don't. Hence my use of the quote, *'fail to prepare, prepare to fail.*

TYPES OF ASSESSMENT EXERCISES

The following are explanations of the various different types of assessments typically used in recruitment today. I've incorporated what they consist of, what the company is testing, and how to prepare (where possible) to successfully achieve the best results.

4

ONLINE TESTS

Online tests are designed to assess many different aspects from your skills/knowledge/experience to your inherent personality traits and may include verbal, numerical, mechanical, psychometrics, etc. Whatever the test is designed to ascertain, here are my top tips:

1. READ THE QUESTIONS CAREFULLY – Candidates tend to skim read questions instead of taking the time to read them thoroughly, and digesting all of the information before answering. The quicker you read, the more chance there is of you misreading something important. Slow your pace down and read the questions out loud or write them on a piece of paper. Make sure you thoroughly understand what you are being asked for before answering.

    Remember in school when you were practising for exams, and your teacher would say, *"Make sure you read and understand the question before writing your answer"*? The same principle applies here.

2. REVIEW YOUR SPELLING – Most candidates don't spend enough time checking their spelling; that indicates to the recruiter that you don't pay attention to detail. Reading your answers out loud as you type them can help you recognise errors.

3. CHECK FOR GRAMMATICAL ERRORS – Some candidates are so concerned about the content of their answers that they forget to follow the correct rules of grammar. Where competition is intense, recruiters are looking for reasons to filter out applicants. If you can't express yourself clearly and accurately when writing, there's less chance that you'll get through to the interview stage or pick up the points you need in an assessment centre.

    Write straightforward sentences that aren't too long or overcomplicated. Reread each sentence after typing it. Look for missing punctuation, sentence fragments, capitalisation errors, sentence run-ons or wordy sentences that you could interpret in different ways. If you have time, write your answers in a word processing application such as MSWord or Apple's Pages. Once you're happy with it, copy and paste the information into the appropriate section online.

4. MANAGE YOUR NERVES – Nerves can affect concentration, resulting in a below-par performance. I've included information on how to handle nerves in Chapter 6. In essence, make sure you eat something to give you energy, visualise performing well and think positively. Use the breathing exercise I've described and read each question carefully which will help take your mind off your nerves.

5. LISTEN TO YOUR GUT INSTINCT – Many candidates make the mistake of doubting themselves and writing what they *think* the recruiter wants to know rather than what they consider to be right. You should always be honest and go with your first gut instinct, that way if you don't get the job, you'll know that the position wasn't right for you and you were being true to yourself.

VIDEO ASSESSMENTS

Video assessments (not to be confused with Skype interviews) are a relatively new assessment technique, increasingly used by larger organisations particularly for graduate and technical roles. They are predominantly another pre-sifting tool used before a face to face interview.

HOW VIDEO ASSESSMENTS WORK

You will usually receive an email from the recruiter containing a link which will take you through to a specially designed website. Here you will be asked a series of questions, which you will need to answer within a set time limit (typically around two minutes each). Answers are video recorded. The difference between this style of assessment and a traditional telephone/Skype or face to face interview is that there won't be an interviewer there to prompt you if you aren't answering the questions thoroughly.

The following are my top tips for this type of assessment:

1. DO YOUR PREPARATION - You should prepare for a video assessment in the same way as you would for a face to face interview using your significant accomplishments in the STAR format (see 'Using the STAR format' in Chapter 2), taking the company's competencies into consideration.

2. PRACTISE YOUR ANSWERS – You may not know the exact questions you'll be asked, but you can have a good guess that they will be about your achievements. Prepare by rehearsing your achievements out loud as many times as possible before the assessment – this is also great practice for when you're subsequently invited to a face to face interview or assessment centre. Again, this is covered in detail in Chapter 2.

3. FIND A QUIET PLACE WHERE YOU WON'T BE INTERRUPTED – This is critical and a top tip from a number of assessors from my research. Make sure you tell the people around you that you must not be disturbed under any circumstances. Not only would it disrupt your concentration if someone were to barge in, but

it will look unprofessional. Whatever you do, DO NOT stop to pet your pooch/cat (I can't believe I have to say that, but apparently, people do!). Remove any pets (and children!) from the room. If you have a dog that consistently barks, put it outside for a while or ask someone to take it for a walk during your assessment.

4. ENSURE THAT YOU AND YOUR ROOM ARE WELL PRESENTED - Although assessors are explicitly told not to take account of what you're wearing or how your surroundings look, those things reflect you/your standards and professionalism. Therefore, both you and the room should look neat and tidy. Remember that whatever you can see on the screen, the assessor can also see. Position yourself in front of a blank wall if you're concerned about your surroundings.

While it isn't necessary to wear a suit, do make sure that you are dressed smart/casual (i.e. no PJs, no slogan T-shirts, inappropriate or dirty/unironed clothing). Comb your hair and make sure that you look presentable. TOP TIP - Remember to look at the camera on your computer /laptop/ phone, not your own picture on the screen, which can be off-putting for the assessor.

5. BE READY TO START STRAIGHT AWAY - Once you log on to the system, you must be prepared to begin the interview straight away, as there's usually no going back once you've clicked the link.

The interview will last for approximately 15-20 minutes and when completed, will be sent to an assessor for marking. The assessor will predominantly look for your thought processes and that you have answered the questions fully.

I have recently heard of another similar type of video interview where you are given a question but are allowed to take as much time as you wish to record your answer. You do this on your phone or laptop and only receive the next question once you've uploaded your video of the previous one, giving you much needed time to think and prepare your answer thoroughly. This means that you can record your replies as many times as you like ensuring that you get it right before submitting; something you aren't otherwise able to do with other types of interview.

The interview instructions should clearly explain which type of interview you will be having. Make sure you read/ listen to any instructions carefully before you start so that you are completely sure of what is required.

PERSONAL OR SUPPORTING STATEMENTS

Personal statements are required less frequently than other forms of assessment but can be needed to supplement your CV or application form. They should not be confused with the 'Summary Statement' at the top of a CV (sometimes also called a 'Personal Statement').

Personal statements frequently form part of internal recruitment processes following organisational restructures. Many of the affected employees may have long service, and, therefore, the organisation already knows their work history, so a CV is not helpful.

A personal statement is a perfect way for the company to find out more about you, especially in areas such as motivation and aptitude for a role. Personal statements are often also required for post-graduate positions where applicants are likely to have limited work experience.

PERSONAL STATEMENT CONTENT

Personal statements provide a chance for you to market your skills, experience and to outline your overall suitability for the role. The company will usually tell you how long your statement should be (up to one page of A4 is typical) and what they want you to cover. Read their guidelines carefully and take the time to plan the structure and content.

You would structure a typical statement in the following way:

1. OPENING - An opening paragraph which starts with a strong statement explaining why you have decided to apply for the role.
2. MIDDLE - Several middle paragraphs which outline your relevant experience, knowledge, skills and interests. You can use some of the achievements from your CV here. Make sure that you refer to the company's competencies (where applicable).
3. END/SUMMARY - A conclusion which sums up what you have to offer and why you think they should consider you for the role.

COMPLETING PERSONAL STATEMENTS

1. Ensure that you carefully read instructions – avoid skim reading as you may miss relevant points/ requirements.

2. For job applications, refer to the job description, person specification and company's competencies/ values/ behaviours and make sure that you write something for each of the essential skills required for the role.

3. Carefully plan out each section of your statement ensuring not only that you cover the key skills, but

also the company's competencies (usually available on their website – see 'Competency Based Interviews' in Chapter 2 for more information on where to source competencies/ values/ behaviours).

4. Write in the first person, e.g. 'I,' 'me,' 'my,' 'we,' 'our,' etc. I recommend that you use 'we' sparingly. When people use the 'we' in an interview/ assessment situation, it can imply that what they've achieved was part of a group effort rather than what the individual has accomplished.

5. Where a word count is stipulated, make sure that you stick to it. If you go over, you will only be marked up to the stipulated word count. The assessor will disregard anything else over and above the allowance stipulated. If you are significantly under the word count, it's likely that you haven't provided enough information.

CHECK YOUR WORK

As with online tests, write straightforward sentences that aren't too long or overcomplicated. Once you've done your initial draft, look for missing punctuation, sentence fragments, capitalisation errors, sentence run-ons or wordy sentences that you could interpret in different ways. Again, it's a good idea to read it out loud which makes it easier to notice sentences that aren't flowing correctly. Once you've made any necessary adjustments and you're happy with what you've written, ask someone else who has a good command of written English, to read it and highlight any errors. It's always difficult for us to notice our own mistakes.

It's also a good idea to run it through a programme such as Grammarly – an online proofreading tool that checks your text for grammar, punctuation, style, etc., which also features a contextual spelling checker and plagiarism detector (Grammarly.com). You can download the basic version for free. The program also highlights where you've used the same word multiple times in the same sentence/ paragraph, and offers suitable alternatives. If you have a PC, download the MS Word add-on which allows you to check your work as you write. If you use a Mac, you can download the app and upload your documents for checking.

PERSONAL STATEMENTS FOR UNIVERSITY APPLICATIONS

Most higher education institutions require a personal statement as part of their selection process. This is a particularly useful tool in this scenario as it's likely that applicants will have minimal relevant experience to include on a CV. As each college/university will tend to have its own requirements, visit their website for clear guidelines on what to cover as well as the suggested word count, which can vary from between 500 to 5,000 words. Again, the format outlined above in Personal Statements, i.e. opening/ middle/ summary will usually suffice. I also recommend following the tips I have included later in this chapter for checking your work.

SITUATIONAL JUDGEMENT TESTS

Situational judgement tests are a type of psychological aptitude test designed to assess your analysis and decision making skills when solving problems in work-related situations. They are usually complete online, without any strict time limits. The company will send an email containing a link that will take you through to the online programme. SJTs are a common selection tool in assessment centres.

With SJTs, you will be given hypothetical and challenging scenarios that you could potentially face on a day-to-day basis in the role. In response to each situation, there will be more than one way to deal with or solve the problem. They are usually presented in a multiple-choice format and consist of up to 50 situations linked to the organisation's competencies.

Depending on the type of test, you will be required to do one of the following:

1. Select both the most effective and least effective response to the situation described.

2. Choose only the most effective response.

3. List the responses in order of effectiveness.

Situational judgement tests have become increasingly popular as assessment tools because they test softer job-related skills that other assessments are unable to measure. They examine practical intelligence and non-academic skills such as problem-solving, decision-making and interpersonal skills, e.g. empathy and how you relate to others. They are frequently used in combination with knowledge-based tests to give a holistic view of a candidate's aptitude for a particular job.

PREPARATION

There is little preparation you can do for SJTs as they are designed to test your general knowledge, ability and life experience. However, I would recommend that you try some practise tests before completing the real thing. Some websites provide these free of charge. Google 'Situational Judgement Tests' and experiment with a few different ones as they do vary depending on the company/ psychologist who's written them.

COMPLETING SJTS

1. Practise, practise, practise! The more practise, the easier the tests will be on the day.

   - Practising will allow you to identify patterns in your responses, e.g. are you a team player or a leader?

   - Only use practice tests that have been designed by qualified Chartered Occupational Psychologists, that way you'll know you've been getting good, quality practice (the website should confirm the designer's qualifications).

2. Read the questions thoroughly and only assign an answer after you've thought carefully about it.

3. Remember that you aren't being asked to judge whether an option is right or wrong, but to evaluate which one you consider being the best (and worst) option(s) available.

4. Don't make assumptions; you must base your responses only on the information provided.

5. When answering the questions, keep the company's competencies in mind and consider the type of role you're applying for and the qualities needed in that role.

6. SJTs aren't usually timed, however, if yours is; remember to keep a close eye on the time – failing to do so may mean that you don't get to finish all the questions, potentially losing out on valuable marks.

7. Answer ALL the questions. Avoid thinking that you'll go back to a question if you're not sure of the answer. Typically, people who do that run out of time and aren't able to go back, again missing out on critical points.

Top Tip - Ask the recruiter if they have any sample questions that you can use as practice. Some may be happy to do this, others may not. However, you don't get if you don't ask!

Psychometric/Personality Testing

These tests are designed to assess your softer, interpersonal skills and behaviours. Often a company will require you to complete such a test before an assessment centre or interview as part of their pre-selection process; however, some will use them on the day.

Psychometric tests are usually conducted online. Again, if you're completing one as an assessment tool before an interview/ assessment centre, it's likely that you will receive an email containing a link to an online portal.

Once you click through to the online assessment tool, you will need to complete approximately 100 questions which will be in a multiple choice or an 'either/or' format. You may find that the same questions are repeated throughout the test, although they may be phrased slightly differently. The different phrasing is intentional, designed to check that you are answering questions truthfully, rather than in the way you *think* you should. These tests are so sophisticated that they will highlight any anomalies in your responses, and generate a score that indicates how truthful you've been.

Once you've completed all the questions, a report will automatically be generated showing your strengths and potential development areas concerning the role you are applying for. It will also provide the recruiter with a range of questions to ask which probe your weaker areas. Unfortunately, there's little preparation you can do for this type of test as they focus on your personality and how you typically behave. However, there are various websites where you can practise example tests for free.

My top tip is to answer as honestly as possible using your first thoughts and your gut feeling. The more you think about a question, usually the harder it will be to answer.

Try not to second-guess the answers you *think* they want because you really don't know! Each type of role requires different personality traits and, therefore, it's wrong to try and second guess what they're looking for. If you do decide to try and manipulate your responses, you are likely to generate an adverse score when it comes to how truthful you've been with your answers, and that will not give a good impression to the recruiter; it is also a strong enough reason to reject your application.

CHAPTER 2 – INTERVIEW PREPARATION

"Thorough preparation makes its own luck."

Face to face interviews are still an integral part of the recruitment process and are relatively easy to prepare for if you know how.

In essence, there are two types of face to face interviews:

1. CV BASED INTERVIEWS – Even though competency interviews are hugely popular, CV based ones are still used as standard in many companies, for both management and non-management roles.

    During CV based interviews, the interviewer may have some pre-prepared questions; however, usually, they will ask you to talk through your CV, asking pertinent questions as you go along.

Although this type of interview is a little more ad-hoc and less structured than competency-based types, **you should still prepare in the same way as you would for competency-based interviews as detailed in this chapter**.

The interview will last anything from half an hour to an hour and a half (the norm being around an hour) depending on the type of role and interviewer. The regular structure of an hour-long interview is:

- Opening by the interviewer - they provide information about the company and background on how the vacancy has arisen (5 minutes)

- The candidate talks through their CV with the interviewer asking relevant questions (40 minutes)

- The candidate asks the interviewer their questions (10 minutes)

- Conclusion to interview including next steps (5 minutes)

There are, however, disadvantages to this type of interview as the process could be seen as unfair. As the questions are unlikely to be structured (i.e. the same questions will not be asked of every candidate), there is an opportunity for what is commonly referred to as 'face fits syndrome'. In other words, the recruiter could pick the person they 'like' the most rather than the one who is most suitable based on qualifications, experience and general personality fit.

This could lead to discrimination claims by applicants, where commence legal action against the company because they perceive that they were rejected because of their race, religion, age, sex, sexual orientation rather than on their skills and experience. Unless the interviewer can clearly evidence their decision making, then the claimant will potentially have an increased chance of winning their case.

2. PANEL/STRUCTURED/COMPETENCY BASED INTERVIEWS – This type of interview is typically used for management, senior management, professional and graduate roles. However, most large companies and public sector organisations use competency-based interviews as their primary assessment method for *all* of their vacancies.

The difference between this style of interview and the CV based version is that every candidate receives the same set of questions. Each answer is marked giving a rating or score based on the quality, according to strict criteria agreed during the interview design stage. The candidate with the highest overall score will usually be offered the role.

There is a caveat here; often companies have a benchmark figure that must be achieved before an offer can be made. For example, the baseline may be set at 75 out of 100, therefore, if none of the candidates achieves a score of 75 or more, they will all be rejected, and the recruitment process will start again.

This type of assessment is appealing to recruiters because:

- It avoids 'face fits,' i.e. giving the position to the person whom the interviewer favours, rather than based on their merits.

- It helps prevent potential discrimination claims as there will be clear, recorded reasons (evidence) to back up the decision-making process, making it harder for rejected candidates to claim that the process was unfair.

However, competency interviews do have their downsides:

- Where the interviewee is particularly nervous, or where they haven't comprehensively prepared (they may not know how to) they may not answer questions thoroughly enough to earn a high enough mark.

- It can be difficult to accurately test the candidate's 'personality fit' with both the company and others within the team. I've witnessed candidates being offered roles because they scored the highest at an interview; however, they didn't quite fit in with the rest of the team and subsequently ended up leaving within their probationary period either by choice or force.

A typical competency-based interview lasts between one and a half and two hours. The structure of a one and a half-hour interview will typically be:

- Opening by the interviewer who provides information on the company and how/ why the vacancy has arisen (10 minutes)

- The interviewer asks the candidate competency-based questions (60 minutes)

- The candidate asks the interviewer their questions (10 minutes)

- Conclusion to interview, including what happens next (10 minutes)

Competency-based interviews also tend to form an integral part of assessment centres, which we'll talk about in more detail later in Chapter 4.

How To Prepare For An Interview

Preparing for any interview is relatively easy; however, it does require time and effort. The thing to remember when you do your preparation is that an interviewer isn't (or shouldn't be) trying to catch you out; they want evidence that you have the right skills, experience, aptitude and behaviours to be successful in the role.

Think of an interview like any other test – you wouldn't turn up for an exam without having done your revision/ preparation, so why would you turn up to an interview without it?

Following are the essential steps that you should following when preparing for any type of interview, i.e. not just competency based.

1. DO YOUR RESEARCH – Make sure that you've thoroughly researched the company. It's so easy to do now that we have everything at our fingertips via the internet. Visit their website and use Google them to find out

any current news stories, social media updates. Not having looked at a company's website is unforgivable. When I interview, I always ask the question, *"What did you think of our website?"* By my reckoning, if someone can't be bothered to look at us, then I can't be bothered to look at them! Many recruiters I spoke to during my research concurred.

You may even consider making a note of a couple of questions to ask them based on what you've seen during your research. A word of caution here; if you choose to raise a question about the company's website (especially if you're interviewing for an IT or marketing role) DON'T CRITICISE IT! Criticising a company's website is a huge mistake that candidates often make and is a sure-fire way to talk yourself out of a job.

If asked you're asked for website feedback, or if there's something that you'd like to know more about it, make sure you phrase it constructively, e.g. *"I like what you did here [ ]. You could expand on that by doing X, Y, Z."* No interviewer will thank you for verbally bashing their website.

2. FOR MANAGEMENT POSITIONS, KNOW THE NUMBERS - This is especially important for senior management/ board roles. Review the company's accounts from

Companies House. It doesn't cost much and will help you prepare more thoroughly. It also looks impressive if you've gone to that much trouble.

Also, **know *your own* numbers,** e.g. your current company's turnover, your budget, your KPIs, etc. Knowing your facts and figures is an absolute must. There's nothing more off-putting for a recruiter than a manager who doesn't know his/her own numbers.

3. IDENTIFY YOUR RELEVANT TRANSFERABLE SKILLS AND ACHIEVEMENTS – Recruiters want to know what's in it for them if they recruit you (WIIFM – What's in It for Me!). Being clear on your transferable skills and how you would use them to best effect is vital. They will also want to hear about your significant achievements in your current/ previous roles. If you've done your CV using the format outlined in Book 3 of the Your Dream Job Series, 'Write a Brilliant CV', you should have already identified them.

4. PREPARE YOUR MAIN ACHIEVEMENTS USING THE STAR FORMAT (described later in this chapter) – Once you have listed your key achievements and I suggest a minimum of eight from the last three years, using the STAR structure is the easiest way of recalling them at interview. That's because they will be in a format that you can easily remember.

5. PRACTISE YOUR ANSWERS (i.e. key achievements) – The more times you practise saying your STAR format answers out loud, the easier it will be to remember them in an interview. When we say something repeatedly out loud, we build strong neural pathways within the brain which makes it easy to access them in stressful/ pressurised situations.

6. PRACTISE TALKING THROUGH YOUR CV/CAREER HISTORY IN FIVE MINUTES – Whether you're having a CV or competency-based interview you need to be able to recite it (without looking if possible) for at least five minutes. You'd be amazed at how many people can't do that. Again, the more times you practise, the easier it will become. Don't be caught out with this one; you will ALWAYS get asked about your CV and your career history.

7. PREPARE QUESTIONS YOU WANT TO ASK – It never ceases to amaze me how so few people have intelligent questions to ask at the end of an interview. Asking quality questions is one of those small things that will make a significant difference to your performance. It may seem unimportant, but if a recruiter has two excellent candidates who have scored equally well and one asks a couple of really great questions, which one do you think will be offered the role? The type of questions you should ask, and more

importantly, those you shouldn't ask, are covered later in this chapter.

Using The S.T.A.R. Format

The STAR format is a universally accepted acronym used for structuring answers to interview questions – especially competency-based questions. You may be thinking, *"But, how do I know what questions they're going to ask me?"* That's simple; **THEY WILL ASK YOU ABOUT YOUR ACHIEVEMENTS** – interviewing isn't rocket science.

If you have followed the advice given in Book 3 of the Your Dream Job Series, 'Write a Brilliant CV', you will already have at least eight achievements from the last three to five years. You will use those examples and break them down into the STAR format.

If you have not read Book 3, you need to give some thought to your most significant achievements from the last three to five years. Here are some guidelines taken from 'Write a Brilliant CV':

- AT LEAST EIGHT TO TEN ACHIEVEMENTS – By achievements I mean the things that you have delivered in your role that have added value to the business. I recognise that this is potentially a new concept for some; many people don't even realise that they have any! However, we all do, no matter what we do, otherwise there would be no point in having the job. People often find it difficult to think about what they've achieved, and when I start to coax it out of them, they'll often say, *"But that's just my job!"*, *"I just do what I do!"*

To clarify, **your achievements are the results or outcomes of your job activities/ duties/ responsibilities**.

To help remind yourself of what you've accomplished:

o ASK YOUR MANAGER – They should be able to tell you.

o ASK YOUR COLLEAGUES – It's likely that they have been part of the same activities or remember what you've been involved in.

o REVIEW YOUR PERFORMANCE MANAGEMENT/ JOB APPRAISALS - Most large companies have a formal appraisal process, and therefore, it is likely that your achievements will be in the documentation. If you don't have a copy of the paperwork, you can usually request it from your manager or HR department.

o LOOK BACK THROUGH YOUR DIARY - What meetings have you attended in the last couple of years? Quite often as soon as we finished a project or a piece of work, we completely forget about it and quickly become engrossed in the next. Looking back through your diary is an excellent way of reminding yourself of what you've been involved with and the achievements that came out of it.

- DEMONSTRATE DIFFERENT ASPECTS OF YOUR ROLE/ YOUR KEY SKILLS – This is where you get the opportunity to demonstrate where your skills and experience match those required for the role.

- TAILOR YOUR ACHIEVEMENTS TO THE VACANCY – Tailoring your achievements is an essential way of showing that you can add value to a prospective employer.

Once you have your eight to ten achievements, you need to break them down into the STAR format.

S.T.A.R.

S – Situation - 10% of the overall answer.

T – Task – 10% of the overall answer.

A – Action – 70% of the overall answer.

R – Result – 10% of the overall answer.

- SITUATION – SET THE SCENE – What was the 'global' or big picture issue, i.e. the wider business problem that had to be solved. The 'Situation' should account for 10% of your answer.

- TASK – WHAT NEEDED TO BE DONE BY YOU – What was *your* role in solving the global issue? What were you tasked with achieving? What was your goal? The 'Task' should account for 10% of your overall answer.

  NOTE - Don't get the 'Task' mixed up with the 'Situation' (many people do). They are different. The Situation is the big picture/ company/ global issue (nothing to do with you), whereas the Task is what you had to do to solve the big problem.

- ACTION – THINKING, SAYING AND DOING – What steps did you take to achieve your goal? To whom did you speak? Where did you visit? What research did you do? Did you manage a team? Did you have a budget? Did you use specific project management techniques? List anything that you had to do, think or say to reach the desired result. Your actions should account for 70% of your overall answer as the recruiter will want to see how you demonstrate your key skills and hear about how you achieve results.

- RESULT – You should clearly define the outcome with tangible evidence. The more facts and figures that you can add in here the better, e.g. money saved/earned, percentages, KPIs, customers gained, customers serviced, business improvements and how the result contributed to the overall success of the organisation. If you've read Book 3 in this series, the 'Result' corresponds with the *so what* test I mentioned in the achievements section of your CV. If you can say, *"so what"* after reading the result/outcome, you haven't written enough. The result should form 10% of your overall answer.

TOP TIP - If you've been part of or managed a large project containing different elements, it's likely that you'll be able to split it down into more than one achievement, demonstrating different competencies.

S.T.A.R. Format Example

The following is a shortened example of the STAR format using my achievement of writing the original 'Land Your Dream Job Now!' book. (NOTE - I haven't written as much as I would if I was preparing for a real interview. My aim here is simply to give you an idea of how to use the STAR structure and what to write under each heading.)

- SITUATION – People looking for a new job don't always know how to go about an effective job search; how to apply for roles or how to successfully manage assessment processes. They also find the whole process particularly nerve-wracking and stressful, especially going for interviews. (*This is the 'global' issue.*)

- TASK - Based on my years of experience as a recruiter and as a career management coach, I decided to write a book that would provide job hunters with the tools and techniques to help them land the job of their dreams. (*This is my role in delivering a solution to the global issue.*)

- ACTION:

  - I reviewed the outplacement and redeployment workshops that my company currently provides to our corporate clients. These workshops include CV writing, job hunting, interview skills, presentation skills, etc.

o   I examined the feedback from workshops to see if there was additional information that I could incorporate into the book.

o   I met with recruitment consultants, in-house recruiters, assessors and HR professionals from my network to clearly understand what recruiters look for during the various assessment types and to discover the common mistakes that candidates make.

o   Using my knowledge and the information I gained through my research, I wrote the book, which also involved designing the accompanying 'additional resources.'

o   I commissioned the book cover and website design.

o   I edited my text and had the book professionally proofread and edited.

o   I designed and implemented a marketing plan to maximise sales.

(These were just some of the actions that I took to achieve the desired result and solve the global issue. You would write everything.)

- RESULT - The book sold over X copies within X months producing revenue of £X to date. As a consequence of the book, 'What Next' has now been commissioned to run career management workshops for new and existing clients with forecast revenue of £X in 2019/2020. *(This is what happened as a result of my actions – notice I've included facts and figures).*

USING THE S.T.A.R. FORMAT

STEP 1

- Choose eight achievements. Use the ones from your CV if you have completed the 'How to Write a Brilliant CV' course (part of the Your Dream Job programme).

- Break substantial achievements into smaller ones, e.g. if you've worked on a significant project with multiple deliverables, it's okay to use those as well as the overall project success.

- Choose ones from within the last 3-5 years, especially if you know that your interview will be competency based. Many recruiters will not accept answers over three years old as they consider them to be out of date.

- HAND WRITE one full page of A4 for each achievement using the S.T.A.R. format. Often clients/delegates want to skip this bit and type up their STAR achievements; that's a mistake. We remember 700% more of what we physically write down. Forcing yourself to write one full page per achievement will create a neural pathway in the brain making the information more accessible when you need it; this is especially so if you practise reading your STAR achievements out loud as many times as possible before an interview.

- Once you've written your achievements in long-hand, allocate the most appropriate competency/value/behaviour to each. If you have a competency-based interview, the company should provide the competencies, or you can usually get them from their website. If you know the meeting will be CV based, you can skip this action.

- Repeatedly practise (role play) reading your achievements out loud. By doing this, you'll strengthen the neural pathway making your examples easier to access when you're in an actual interview situation.

STEP 2

Once you've written your eight achievements in long-hand, edit your full-page achievements into easy to remember bullet points:

- Take 4 pieces of A4 paper and split them in half horizontally.

- Jot down two achievements (in the STAR format) per page using as few words as possible (just enough to jog your memory should you need it - don't use shorthand that you may forget it you're under pressure).

- If you know you'll be having a competency-based interview, write the competency/value/behaviour at the top of each achievement (see Competency Based Interviews later in this chapter).

- Either use very big handwriting or type in a huge font.

- Alternatively, use index cards - one achievement per card

WRITING YOUR ACHIEVEMENTS IN THE STAR FORMAT IS THE MOST CRITICAL PART OF YOUR INTERVIEW PREPARATION – IF YOU DECIDE NOT TO DO IT, THEN YOU CAN'T EXPECT TO ACHIEVE EXCEPTIONAL RESULTS.

```
Competency: Put the customer first


Situation: People poor at interviews
Task: Help them
Action: Research, workshop, support, etc.
Outcome: 100% jobs, 3 months
_____

Competency: Creating Innovation


Situation: Lack of on-line training for CVs
Task: Design an on-line programme
Action: Research, workshop, record, deliver
Outcome: 1000 sign ups - £ revenue
```

COMPETENCY BASED INTERVIEWS

You should use the STAR format to prepare for ALL interviews, no matter what the type. However, it's particularly important to use this system for competency interview preparation. If you're in doubt about the kind of interview you'll be having, don't be afraid to ask the recruiter, they should be happy to tell you.

If you are to have a competency-based interview, you should request a copy of the competencies that you are going to be assessed against (sometimes called 'values' or 'behaviours' depending on the company).

If they don't provide you with a copy, you can usually find them on the organisation's website. Search for 'Company Values', 'Our Values', 'Core Values', 'Behaviours' or 'Competencies' or look for the company's mission statement and you'll usually find them alongside.

WHAT ARE COMPETENCIES/CORE VALUES?

Competencies or core values are the guiding principles that define how an organisation behaves. Competencies/ core values help companies determine if they are on the right path and fulfilling their business goals; and they create a guide which all employees, clients, and providers should be aware of.

The following is a short list of typical company values/ competencies:

- Honesty
- Respect
- Customer first
- Staff development
- Innovation
- Creativity

- Courageousness
- Commitment

Top Tip - **Once you've written your eight achievements in long-hand, carefully read the company's competencies and assign the most appropriate one for each of your achievements**. For example, if I was preparing for an interview with a company who had the same competencies as I've listed above, I could say my 'book' achievement demonstrated 'Innovation' and 'Creativity.' If I were then asked a question about being creative or innovative, I'd be able to give my 'book' example to demonstrate how I met competency.

It's possible that you will find that two or three competencies fit any one of your achievements. If that's the case, try not to repeat yourself by using the same example more than once. That's why I suggest that you prepare at least eight achievements. If the company has more than eight competencies (unlikely, but possible), then you'll need to come up with more achievements to illustrate them.

Competency Based Questions

As I've already mentioned, competency-based questions are designed to test where your knowledge, experience and aptitude match the company's competencies, and you will be scored based on the quality of your answers.

When the recruiter is creating the questions, they will make a list of all the elements that make an answer excellent, mediocre or a fail. Depending on your replies, they will assign a score based on how what you say matches against their benchmark.

Typical competency-based questions start with:

"Give me an example of a time when you've had to..."

'"Tell me when you've delivered..."

"When did you last have experience of...?"

Going back to my 'book' example and the competency of creativity, I may be asked, *"Give me an example of when you have done something creative (or innovative) that has added value."* I would then give them my answer using the STAR format I'd prepared.

ANSWERING INTERVIEW QUESTIONS

It's fine to respond to questions referring to the STAR format, for example:

"The situation was..."

"My task was..."

"The action I took was..."

"The results were…"

No good interviewer will have a problem with you doing that. It's also an excellent way to stay on track if you know that you occasionally wander and get a bit lost when answering questions. It's relatively common for interviewees to forget the question halfway through their answer. Using the STAR format will help to keep you on track.

I strongly urge you to take your STAR format bullet notes (Step 2 above) into interviews, especially if you know that you get nervous or tend to go 'blank.' The majority of my clients find that they never need to refer to their notes, but just knowing that they have them to fall back on, if necessary, is a big comfort.

TAKING NOTES TO INTERVIEWS

1. IF YOU DO NEED TO REFER TO YOUR NOTES, ASK THE INTERVIEWER FIRST – Say something like, *"I haven't had an interview for a while, and so I took the initiative and wrote some notes to bring with me. Do you mind if I refer to them?"* Very few interviewers will say no, and if they do, you have to ask yourself if that's the kind of company for whom you wish to work. Don't ask at the beginning of the interview as it sets the wrong tone; only ask when/if you need to.

If a candidate does ask to look at their notes, it tells the recruiter that they know their weaknesses, and they have taken steps to address them. All the recruiters/ assessors I've spoken to about this topic, totally agree on this.

2. MAKE SURE YOU SPACE YOUR NOTES OUT – Type them using a large font or use neat large block handwriting that can be read without difficulty when you're under pressure, we tend not to be able to see clearly when we're in stressful situations.

3. **DO NOT** TAKE YOUR LONGHAND NOTES WITH YOU - You will never be able to read them in a pressurised environment, and it will have the opposite effect than what you would hope; making you more look and feel flustered and out of control.

With all the clients I've personally coached through the career management process, I can only recall two needing to look at their notes. The first completely ignored my advice about just using bullet point notes and proceeded to tie himself up in knots as he tried desperately to read his long-hand achievements. He didn't get the job.

The second hadn't had an interview for approximately thirty years and happened to lose his way during an answer. He asked the interviewer if he could review his notes, which he did briefly with their consent, enabling him to get back on track quickly. The feedback from the interviewer was they were impressed with his preparation which contributed toward their decision to offer him the role.

Top Ten Most Frequently Asked Questions

As well as competency-based questions, there are also frequently asked questions for which you should prepare answers. **They don't need to be in the STAR format**; however, you should give them some serious thought and jot down ideas of how you would answer them.

Every single client that my colleagues and I have worked with in a career management capacity has been asked at least two of these questions at every interview:

1. **"Tell me about yourself/Talk me through your CV"** – The interviewer is saying *"I want to hear you speak."* These are common questions to get the interview started and put you at ease. Be able to talk through your CV, your personal attributes and qualifications in around five minutes, emphasising the experience and skills that are relevant to the job.

2. **"What are your strengths?"** – The interviewer wants a straightforward answer as to what you are good at and how you're going to add value. Your strengths

lie in the skills you have that will separate you from other candidates, so list three or four and explain how they would benefit the employer. Strengths to consider include technical proficiency, determination to succeed, positive attitude, the ability to learn quickly, the capacity to relate to people and achieve a common goal. You may be asked to give examples of the above so be prepared.

3. ***"What are your weaknesses/ development areas?"*** – The interviewer is asking about your self-perception and self-awareness. **DON'T GIVE THEM A REASON NOT TO EMPLOY YOU!** Asking about your weaknesses or development areas is another standard question for which you can be well prepared. N.B. it's not appropriate to say that you don't have any as everyone has growth areas; no matter how good they are at their job.

You have two options when answering this type of question. The first is to use a weakness such as a lack of experience (not ability) in an area that is not vital for the job, and tell them how you would go about addressing it.

The second option is to describe a weakness that could also be considered as a strength and the steps you would take to combat it. An example would be,

"Attention to detail is important to me, and I can't afford information to go out from my team that isn't correct as it could cost the company thousands of pounds. I realised that I was becoming a bottleneck because I wanted to check everything personally, which was starting to affect deadlines. I, therefore, put a new process in place where my team checks each other's work before it goes out. That way I'm no longer a bottleneck, and we are continuing to hit our deadlines."

Do not select a personal weakness such as *"I'm not a morning person. However, I'm much better as the day goes on."* That's a real example of how a candidate answered that question! Again, don't give the recruiter a reason not to employ you.

4. **"What's the biggest mistake you've made and how did you correct it?"** - The interviewer is trying to find out your definition of 'a mistake' and whether you show a logical approach to problem-solving using your initiative. Give them an example of something small. Describe how you defined the problem, what the options were, why you selected the solution you did and what the outcome was. Always end on a positive note. NOTE - you may also be asked what you would do differently next time.

5. ***"How do you like to be managed?"*** - The interviewer wants to find out whether you can work on your own initiative or whether you need close supervision. The perfect way to answer this question is, *"I like to be left to get on with my job but know that there's support there if I need it."* This statement will give the recruiter confidence that you're not high maintenance and get things done without the need to be micro-managed.

6. ***"How would your colleagues or manager describe you?"*** – It never ceases to amaze me how people are still surprised when they get asked this question, as it's fairly standard. The correct answer would be, *"I think that they would describe me as trustworthy, honest and supportive and a team player"* or *"honest, hardworking, conscientious"* etc. Again, reflect on the type of person the recruiter is looking for, and then choose which adjectives that best describe you. Remember to check the company's competencies or person specification, if they are available, and tailor your answer to those.

7. ***"What don't you like about your current job?"*** – Be careful how you respond to this one. There are always aspects of our jobs that we dislike; so, it's not appropriate to say *"nothing."* Choose something small and inconsequential or something that you

don't like doing, but you've found a way to make it enjoyable or even fun.

8. **"What's the reason for leaving your current employer?"** – The interviewer is trying to understand and evaluate your motives for moving. If you're leaving of your own accord, state that you're looking for a new challenge, more responsibility, the opportunity to gain additional experience or a change of environment, etc. Avoid being negative and never cite 'salary' as the primary motivator.

If you have been made redundant, say so. It's no reflection on you or how you did your job, so don't try to cover it up. Be open and explain the company's reasons for the restructure, remember that it was your *job* that was made redundant, not you.

9. **"Why do you want to work here?"** - The interviewer wants to find out just how much you know about the company and the role. They want evidence that the job suits you, fits in with your general aptitudes, coincides with your long-term goals and involves things you enjoy doing. Make sure you have a good understanding of the role and the organisation and describe what is attracting you to the role/ company. Use information from the company's website to get a

good feel for their culture, products, services, social responsibility, etc.

10. ***"Why should we give the job to you?"*** – I ask this question at every interview without fail, because if you don't know why a company should recruit you, then how would they know? It's a question that many native Britons find difficult to answer, typically because we tend to be told not to brag about our achievements as we grow up, resulting in many of us feeling uncomfortable when forced to tell a prospective employer how good we are. The problem with that is if you don't tell them, the next person will. Your answer to this question could mean the difference between landing the job or not.

An excellent reply to this would be, *"You should recruit me because I think I'm an excellent fit with your company and the role, not just because of my skills and experience, but because of culture and values too.   I know I can do a brilliant job for you, and I'd relish the opportunity to make a difference."*   Sounds a bit cheesy, but it's what a recruiter wants to hear.

MANAGERS MAY ALSO GET ASKED:

11. ***"How do you like to manage?"*** - The assessor wants to find out whether you like to control everything

around you (micro-manage) or whether you're more easy-going. A good way to answer this question is, *"I like to leave my staff to get on with their jobs, but know that I'm here to support them if they need me."* Followed by, *"I like to set clear goals with achievable timescales so that my team knows what I expect of them. I regularly check in with them to ensure that they are managing their workload and deadlines effectively".*

12. **"What do you think your priorities will be in the first three months?"** – Here, the interviewer is looking to see if you've grasped the main elements of the role as well as the potential problems. They are interested in hearing how you will evaluate, plan and organise your time including, how you would get to know the business, understand the challenges and start to prepare for the future.

13. **"How do you manage stress"** – Most management roles are stressful. Therefore, the recruiter will want to know what you do to relieve stress and how you handle demanding situations. If you get asked this question, they will be looking for two things, utilisation of your skills (organising, planning, delegating, etc.) as well as what you physically do outside work to manage stress (exercise, holidays, hobbies, etc.).

HOBBIES AND INTERESTS

It's likely that the recruiter will ask you about your hobbies and interests. Be careful with this one and give it some thought before the interview. As I discuss in book 3 of this series, 'Write a Brilliant CV' when deciding on what to include in the 'Additional Information' section of your CV, companies like candidates who have hobbies and interests that align with their values.

Therefore, try to have something interesting to talk about that matches the values of the company. It should be current, not something you've done in the dim and distant past. Interviewers like applicants who:

- Are involved with charities.

- Are involved in sports.

- Are involved with 'clubs' e.g. running/ painting/ football/ Scouts/ Guides/ Brownies/ Cadets etc.

- Are studying – undertaking further education.

- Have a non-paid role outside their regular job, e.g. school governor, councillor, non-executive director.

- Are fluent in another language.

I recently heard of a candidate who went for an interview with a forward-thinking company who only recruit people with drive, ambition and who want to make a difference. She had done a fantastic interview and ticked all the boxes with her exemplary answers, only to completely blow her chances at the last hurdle. As she was being escorted out of the building, the recruiter asked her about her plans for the weekend. Without thinking, she replied, *"I'll be having a complete chill out this weekend, you know, onesie and a full-on Netflix binge."*

Up until that point, the recruiter was planning to offer her the role. However, her weekend plans were the complete opposite of what he would expect from the type of person that would fit with their culture, and that was enough of a reason for him to reject her.

Top Tip - You should avoid the common hobbies/interests that everyone *thinks* that they should say, e.g. cinema, socialising, reading. Everyone does those, and they say little about you.

Whatever hobbies/interests you decide to use:

- **They must be current - you must be doing them now**. Something that you *used* to do is likely to be irrelevant today.

- **It must be the truth** – Don't say something if you don't do it. I've caught people lying when I've asked about their hobbies. I'll ask what the last film was that they saw if they tell me that they like going to the cinema. I'm a massive film fan, and I know what's showing at the movies most of the time. If an interviewee can't answer me quickly or if they can't give me a recent film, I'll think they're lying.

That goes for 'reading' too. I'll ask a candidate what they're currently reading or who their favourite author or genre is, often, they can't answer.

Lying about your hobbies and interests and getting caught out will throw everything else you've said into question, which can mean that you fail an otherwise excellent interview.

- **Use the same examples as you gave on your CV** (if you added this section – my advice is not to include it unless you have something interesting/ out of the ordinary to say) - It's common for anything you've listed in your 'additional information' to be explored during an interview.

YOUR QUESTIONS FOR THEM

The questions you ask during an interview are much more critical than most candidates give them credit for. You may think that they make up such a small part of the interview process, that they can't have a substantial bearing on the outcome. However, if you're in direct competition with another candidate and there's little to differentiate between the two of you, the questions you ask can make all the difference.

Your chance to ask the recruiter questions tends to be at the end of the interview, and unfortunately, by this point, most candidates are a bit tired, a little 'wrung out' and just want to get out of there. Therefore, for many, when asked if they have any questions, there can be a temptation to say, *"No thank you. You've answered everything as we've gone along."* I'm always disappointed when I get this response; it's just not acceptable.

TOP TIP - Make a list of around ten, quality questions and take them to the interview with you. That's not to say that you'll ask all ten, you will probably be given time to pose around two or three at most. However, preparing more will provide you with options in case some are answered during the interview.

Your typed questions should be in extra-large print and well-spaced out on a sheet of A4 paper so that you can read them without difficulty when you're under pressure. We can find it difficult to read small type print with tight line spacing when we're stressed. When the interviewer asks if you have any questions, you can produce the sheet from your nicely presented folder and ask anything significant that's still outstanding.

Planning your questions beforehand not only shows the interviewer that you are prepared, but it ensures that you ask quality questions rather than frantically searching around for something on the spare of the moment, or even worse, not having anything to ask.

Interviews are a two-way process – you need to be sure that the job is right for you, every bit as much as the company knowing you're a 'fit' for them. Asking quality questions is your chance to interview the company, obtaining answers that you need to help you to make the right decision if you're subsequently offered the role.

Here are some generic questions that work well:

- *"How could I impress you in my first three months?"* - The answer to this will tell you how they would like to see you perform and the areas where you should be concentrating if you were successful. It also shows the recruiter that you're thinking ahead and want to do what's best for the company as well as for yourself.

- *"What challenges could I face in the first three months?"* - It's worth being aware of anything that may stop you from reaching your objectives. The fact that you're asking about them at the interview shows that you're aware of that possibility and want to work through or around them to succeed.

- **"Is there anything you would like to improve in your department and how could I help?"** – Asking this shows that you're keen to be part of the team from day one and contribute to the broader goals of the department and the broader company.

- **"What's the working environment like?"** or **"How would you describe the company's culture?"** – If the interviewer hasn't covered this area during the interview, ask about it. It'll help you understand if you would fit in. Make sure what they tell you fits in with your expectations and your requirements.

- **"Will I receive any development in the role?"** – It's important to find out what sort of opportunities there are for promotion in future (if that's important to you) and to ask it without coming across as if you want to leap into a more senior job before you've got this one. It also shows the interviewer you're committed to learning and growing within the company.

The following is a list of other excellent questions:

- *"How/why has the position become available?"*

- *"Can you describe my area of responsibility?"*

- *"How does the role/department fit into the structure of the organisation as a whole?"*

- *"Who will I be reporting to?"*

- *"How would you describe your company's culture?"*

- *"How will my performance be evaluated?"*

- *"Is there a clearly defined career path?"*

- *"What would I be expected to do on a typical day?"*

- *"What do you like about working here?"* (I really like that question, as it turns the emphasis back on the recruiter and will make them think.)

Of course, you may have some questions of your own from your research around the job content or organisation. You should ask ones that are important to you.

At the end of the interview, you should remember to ask:

- **"What are the next stages and when can I expect to hear about the outcome?"** – It can sometimes take a while for hiring managers to come to a decision, and that can be frustrating. Hearing about whether you've got a job, or not, maybe *everything* to you; however, it's only one of many tasks for the recruiter. Try to find out potential dates for further interviews/ assessment centres or some indication that they want to take your application further.

You shouldn't use this question in place of any of the ones mentioned earlier. Despite what many candidates think and some career advisers suggest, it doesn't say anything positive about you and your thought processes – it is a secondary question. Therefore, while it is important, it should be left until the very end of the interview.

QUESTIONS **NOT** TO ASK

Of course, there are also some things that you should *never* ask, these include:

- **Anything to do with pay (especially sick pay!)** – At the beginning of my HR career, I interviewed hundreds if not thousands of candidates for Warehouse Operative positions. I remember one candidate asking about the company's sick pay scheme. What that screams to a recruiter is: *"I INTEND TO BE OFF SICK ... A LOT! HOW MUCH WILL I GET PAID?"*

- *"What days/hours will I be working?"*

- *"Will I have to work on weekends?"*

- *"Is there a bonus scheme?"*

- *"Can I work from home?"*

- *"What does your company do?"*

- *"What's this job for again?"*

- *"When can I take time off for a holiday?"*

- *"How long would I have to wait to get promoted?"*

- *"How long is the lunch break?"*

- *"Does this company monitor Internet usage?"*

- *"How many warnings do you get before you get sacked?"*

- *"Did I get the job?"*

(All the above are real-life examples of candidate questions provided by recruiters during my research.)

I realise it may be vital for you to know the answers to some of these questions. However, anything to do with hours, shifts, weekend working, pay and benefits, etc., you should find those out **BEFOREHAND** (that is unless you've been told that they will be discussed during the interview). We all know that we go to work for money, and it's essential to have a good work/life balance. However, if you ask anything about money/ hours, etc. the recruiter will think that's all you're bothered about, which may well be true; however, you shouldn't let them know that. Every company likes to think that you want to work for them because they're such a fabulous employer, and that's what you should leave them believing.

TOP TIP - It's much better to negotiate the salary, benefits, hours, etc. when you get offered the role. You're in a much stronger position then because the employer is 'bought in' to you. They've also potentially spent a lot of money getting to the offer stage and therefore, at this point you'll find it's much easier to negotiate the package you want. There's more information regarding Job Offers in book 5 of the Your Dream Job series, 'Managing the Job Offer Process'.

SECOND INTERVIEWS

You will have done the majority of the preparation needed for a second interview when you prepared for the first. While your second interview may be with a different interviewer, you can't leave that to chance. Even if they are different interviewers, it's likely that they'll have a copy of the initial interview notes, especially if it was a competency-based interview. Therefore, expect some repetition from the first, but try to keep answers fresh.

Second Interview Preparation

1. Review your performance from the first interview – Be self-critical about what went well and what could be improved on. Take time to work on anything you think needs to be adjusted.

2. Identify any material you didn't cover – Make a note of any preparation that you didn't use in the first interview. Rather than repeating yourself, it's always good to introduce new information, examples, and achievements at the second interview.

3. Find out the type of interview you'll be having – Ask whether you will have a competency or CV based interview.

4. Prepare new examples especially for competency-based interviews – If you used all your achievements in the first interview, write some new ones (you may want to consider using ones from a previous role, preferably where the position was within the last three years).

5. Carry out more research – Review what you were told about the company in the first interview. Is there any more research you can do based on what you learnt? Do you know anyone who works there? If so, try and speak to them to get an insider view of

culture, current 'hot topics,' buzzwords and the types of questions to ask that will impress.

6. PREPARE YOUR QUESTIONS FOR THEM – Ask any questions that didn't get answered in the first interview, but also include any that you may have on reflection.

Chapter 3 - Telephone/Skype Interviews

"The only place where success comes before work is in the dictionary."

Many candidates tend not to prepare adequately for a telephone/Skype interview, often affording it less importance than a face to face meeting. However, they are usually the first step in an assessment process and as such are equally as important as any other selection method.

For both telephone and Skype interviews, you should prepare in exactly the same way as you would for a face to face interview, e.g.:

1. Do your research on the company.

2. Prepare your STAR format achievements.

3. Be able to talk about your CV in five minutes.

4. Prepare your answers to the top ten most asked interview questions – top thirteen if you're applying for a management role.

5. Give some thought to your hobbies and interests which match with the company's values.

6. Prepare your questions to ask the interviewer.

Other top tips that apply to both Skype and telephone interviews:

1. USE A QUIET ROOM WHERE YOU WON'T BE INTERRUPTED – If you're at home and the family are around, ask them to go out for an hour during your call. There's nothing worse than having someone barge in on you when you're right in the middle of explaining the key aspects of your role.

2. MAKE SURE YOU'RE AVAILABLE WHEN THE CALL COMES IN – It's incredibly annoying when a recruiter calls a candidate only to receive an engaged tone or no answer at all. There's no difference between that and turning up late for an interview.

3. REMOVE ANY PETS FROM THE ROOM – As I mentioned when I discussed Video Assessments in Chapter 1. This was a top tip from a recruitment consultant

friend of mine. She said that it's incredibly annoying and off-putting (not to mention unprofessional) when a candidate stops an interview to talk to their pet!

4. HAVE THE RIGHT INFORMATION TO HAND – You should have your CV, the job description, person specification, your key achievements in the STAR format, the company's competencies and your questions for the interviewer in front of you. The great thing about telephone interviews is that the recruiter can't see you referring to your notes.

5. ENSURE RESPONSES ARE CLEAR, CONCISE AND SUCCINCT – If you've done your interview preparation, and you've practised saying your achievements in the STAR format, out loud numerous times, then this shouldn't be a problem. Keep answers short and to the point and avoid waffling.

6. REMEMBER TO ASK *"WHAT HAPPENS NEXT?"* – Quite often candidates are so glad that the interview is over that they forget to ask about the next steps. You should try to find out what to expect afterwards, before the end of the call.

Telephone Interviews

There are distinct differences between phone, Skype and face to face interviews. The following are my top tips for phone interviews:

1. IF YOU'RE IN THE CAR, PULL OVER – Don't have the conversation while you're driving. It's not professional, and you'll never be able to give the interviewer (or your driving) the attention they deserve. If you have to take the call while you're out and about, make sure that you're parked up in a safe place, at least five minutes before the interview start time.

2. STAND UP AND WALK AROUND – If possible, you should always stand up and walk around. *Motion creates emotion*; therefore, if you're on your feet, you'll be much more animated which you will reflect in your voice.

3. PAY EXTRA ATTENTION TO WHAT THE INTERVIEWER IS ASKING – When we can't see the other person, we are unaware of their body language (words are only 7% of our overall communication, 56% of how we communicate is through our body language). Therefore, if you're unsure what the interviewer

68

means, don't be afraid to ask for clarification or for the question to be repeated.

4. KNOW WHEN TO KEEP QUIET – In an interview, it's not up to you to fill silences. Just because the interviewer is silent when you've finished giving an answer does not indicate that you have to fill the space with waffle! Know when to stop. If the interviewer is quiet, it usually means that they are writing notes; it's not a cue for you to keep talking. I've seen so many candidates ruin perfectly good answers because they don't know when to stop. Stick to your STAR format and don't be tempted to add more to fill the silence, let the interviewer do that.

SKYPE/BLUEJEANS INTERVIEWS

Many recruiters, especially recruitment consultants, now use Skype or Bluejeans (business video conferencing) as a pre-sifting tool, before an expensive formal face to face interview. It's particularly useful where the candidate and assessor are based in different locations; it is a cost-effective way of interviewing.

Again, you should prepare for a Skype interview as you would for a face to face meeting. However, there are some top tips you should consider, which are similar to those I outlined in the 'Video Assessment' section in Chapter 1.

1. CHECK YOUR APPEARANCE – Although it's not necessary to wear a suit, you should ensure that you look neat and professional. Wear a shirt/blouse and your hair should be neat and tidy. DO NOT wear sportswear, anything revealing or too casual, e.g. slogan t-shirts.

2. BE MINDFUL OF YOUR SURROUNDINGS – Even though the assessor shouldn't take the room behind you into consideration, if it is dirty, messy or you have inappropriate posters on the walls, it won't give a professional image. Position your computer/ phone/ tablet/ phone in a way that you are in front of a blank wall. What you see on the screen is what the assessor can see.

3. HAVE AN 'APPROPRIATE' SKYPE NAME – Avoid using nicknames or anything that could be classed as offensive.

4. CHECK THAT THE TECHNOLOGY IS WORKING – There's nothing more frustrating for a recruiter than arranging time in their busy schedule to talk to a candidate, only to find that their Skype isn't working. Try it out with a friend beforehand so that you're ready to go at the allotted time.

5. LOOK INTO THE CAMERA ~ Candidates tend to look at the little picture of themselves displayed on the screen rather than looking into the camera lens. Looking at your own picture appears very odd to the assessor and has the same effect as not looking someone in the eye, so make sure you address the camera rather than your own image.

Chapter 4 - Assessment Centres

"Before anything else, preparation is the key to success."

It's increasingly common for companies to use assessment centres for management, senior management, graduate and professional roles (e.g. IT, Sales, HR, and Marketing). Many organisations consider selection centres to be the best way to test a candidate's all-around skills, knowledge, experience including their interpersonal skills against the company's competencies/values.

Large corporations and public sector organisations, including many charities, councils, and NHS tend to use assessment centres for most of their vacancies no matter what the level or role.

Assessment centres can last anything from a couple of hours to a couple of days and consist of a selection of exercises or tasks which are scored in much the same way as competency-based interviews. The candidate with the highest overall score at the end of the assessment is usually the one who is offered the job, provided that they hit the benchmark figure.

As discussed when we covered competency-based interviews, assessment centres are designed to find the right overall person for the role and to avoid 'face fits' syndrome or any potential claims of discrimination.

For management, professional or graduate positions, candidates will often be provided with information based on a fictitious, but similar company. This information can include documentation relating to an overview of the company, performance data, customer satisfaction surveys, etc. The assessors will base the assessment exercises on that information.

Using a fictitious company is the closest way a recruiter has of determining how you would manage similar situations, tasks, and interactions in a real-life scenario. However, this isn't always the case. Some companies base their assessments loosely on related everyday activities that you would encounter within their own organisation.

Before attending an assessment centre, it's essential to have a copy of the company's competencies so that you are aware of the criteria you will be assessed against. You can obtain one by either asking the recruiter or downloading them from the company website. See Chapter 2 for more information on competencies.

OVERNIGHT STAYS/DINNER/DRINKS

Where an assessment centre is based over two days, it's often the case that you will be invited to a dinner or drinks. Spending social time with the candidates is not merely something arranged by recruiters for practical reasons; it is an integral part of the selection process.

In a social setting, the assessors get first-hand experience of how candidates interact on a personal level. Often, senior managers/ directors who are not involved directly in the assessments will attend evening activities to meet the candidates and better assess their personality 'fit' for the organisation. It also enables candidates to ask the management team questions, allowing them to learn more about the culture, values, goals and aspirations of the business from those who actually run it.

TOP TIPS - For ensuring you make a good impression in social assessment situations:

1. DON'T GET DRUNK! – If you do drink alcohol, having a couple is fine, that's being sociable. However, getting drunk is totally unacceptable. Unfortunately, I've witnessed candidates having too much to drink and either causing a scene or making a fool of themselves, only to have to face the assessment team and the other candidates the next morning.

    Make no mistake; the dinner/ drinks are every bit as much a part of the selection process as the formal exercises. If you fail this 'test', you will, without a doubt, fail the entire assessment – no matter how well you do with everything else.

2. KEEP YOUR VIEWS ABOUT THE OTHER CANDIDATES OR THE ASSESSORS TO YOURSELF – Don't ever get drawn into gossiping about other candidates or the assessors. You never know who may overhear or who may relay your views to the assessors (it is a competitive environment so don't be lulled into a false sense of security).

3. DON'T 'SUCK UP' TO THE ASSESSORS/ MANAGEMENT TEAM – Be polite and engaging, ask questions and show interest. However, don't try and monopolise a person's time. It will annoy them and is likely to have the opposite effect to what you were hoping to achieve. There have been times when managers

have asked me to 'save' them from overbearing candidates. You don't want to be remembered for the wrong reason.

4. TAKE NOTE OF THE DRESS CODE – Usually, the dress code for dinner/ drinks is smart/ casual. That means no trainers, t-shirts, vests, sportswear. For men, that means dark, clean jeans/chinos (no light, faded or ripped jeans), dark trousers are good too, paired with an open-necked shirt and a jacket. Ladies, please ensure that you don't dress provocatively with too much skin on show. A smart dress or dark jeans/ skirt/ trousers with a neat blouse/ shirt is acceptable.

    If in doubt, ask about the dress code and examples of what that means. I always prefer people to ask rather than turn up unprepared. Remember they are assessing how you present yourself in a more casual environment and whether you still remain professional. This gives the recruiter a good indication of how you would behave if you were representing the company externally and out of hours.

5. PREPARE SOMETHING INTERESTING TO SAY – If you know that you're uncomfortable in social situations, plan some topics to talk around and casually drop them into the conversation as and when you think it's

appropriate. An excellent way to build rapport is to assume you already have it, talking to people as if you've known them for a while. Another great tip is to make the conversation entirely about the other person. On the whole, people like to talk about themselves, so if you focus your questions around them, it will take the pressure off you.

6. USE THE OPPORTUNITY TO NETWORK – If you do feel a bit uncomfortable, you may have a tendency not to circulate, preferring instead to stay with one or two people with whom you feel at ease. However, that won't help you in this scenario. Make sure that you work your way around the room and talking to as many people as possible. If you don't speak to a representative of the company, they will notice or even worse; they won't see you at all. Building relationships with the right people, but without monopolising their time, is crucial.

ASSESSMENT CENTRE EXERCISES

Following is a list of the most typical assessment centre activities and how to manage them effectively:

GROUP TASK

The group task is performed with other candidates and is an excellent way to get a feel for your competition. It's a common misapprehension that the most vocal, pushy person, who immediately takes the lead, forcing their opinion on others, will score the most points during this task. This couldn't be further from the truth. The assessors will mark you on your contribution to the group's overall achievement and how you demonstrate your skills that match the company's competencies for example:

- LISTENING SKILLS – Whether you are able to hear and understand instructions. I've witnessed many group tasks fail because candidates don't pay attention to the outcomes required. The assessors will also want to see whether you listen to your colleagues and if you take their views/ suggestions into account.

- HOW YOU WORK WITH AND RELATE TO OTHERS – If you can collaborate with a team but also how you lead if that's a skill required in the role. They will want to see you demonstrate that you are supportive of your teammates.

- THE BALANCE BETWEEN YOUR CONTRIBUTION AND VALUING OTHERS – They will test whether you can get your point across without bullying or forcing your opinion on others and whether you encourage them to talk about their ideas as well as your own.

- BEING ASSERTIVE BUT NOT OVERBEARING – It's important to show your leadership skills. However, being a leader does not mean ignoring others' opinions and asserting your own. Be mindful of other peoples' opinions.

- INVITING QUIETER MEMBERS TO JOIN IN – This is of crucial importance, especially in leadership positions. You should encourage the quieter, more reserved individuals to join in. They are usually the 'thinkers' of the group, the ones that tend to consider everything before jumping in head first. They can be invaluable in a team effort as they usually take into consideration the issue as a whole and see problems that others who rush in, may not.

- DON'T VOLUNTEER TO BE THE SCRIBE/NOTE TAKER - Most people think that they look proactive if they nominate themselves to take the group's notes. However, the scribe is usually too busy writing to be able to take a fully active part in completing the task – **if you don't participate actively, you will receive fewer marks**.

If you do decide to scribe, don't use a flip chart; write from a position within the group. Once you remove yourself, which you automatically do when standing up, you'll be less involved and unlikely to be included critical decisions, making it almost impossible to receive a good score.

- AVOID PERFORMING THE ROLE OF FACILITATOR – Again, it's difficult for the assessors to mark you when you're facilitating and not taking an active part in tasks.

- KEEP FOCUS ON THE TIME – Especially if you nominate yourself or are appointed as the timekeeper. Another reason most group exercises fail is due to a lack of time management (even where there is a timekeeper!). Often, team members get so involved with solving the problem that they forget about the time altogether. Everyone in your team will lose points if you go over time and don't manage to complete the task.

PRESENTATIONS

During presentations, you are being tested not just your technical ability, but how you prepare, work under pressure, your communication skills and if you're able to speak in public with confidence. Presentations are covered in detail in Chapter 5.

Psychometric Testing

Psychometric tests are used to measure your thought processes and personality. Often psychometric testing will take place during an assessment centre rather than as a pre-selection tool. For further details, see Chapter 1.

Verbal/Numerical/Technical/Mechanical Testing

These tests assess your aptitude for Maths and English as well as your technical abilities required for the role. Again, you will complete them online as one of a number of tasks throughout an assessment centre. See 'Online Testing' in chapter 1 for more information.

In-Tray Exercise

There are many examples of in-tray exercises. In essence, they consist of a piece of work which deliberately relates to something you would be required to do in the role. For example:

- An accountant may be given an exercise that involves data analysis.

- A PA could be required to write a formal letter.

- A salesperson could be asked to devise a sample sales plan.

- A designer may create a piece of artwork.

There's little preparation you can do for in-tray exercises. However, remember to read the instructions carefully and stick to time. Avoid trying to plan everything in rough (although an outline is fine) as you may run out of time, which is a common mistake often made by candidates. My top tip is to clearly establish your desired **outcome** from the outset. Everything you then do should refer back to your outcome.

ROLE PLAY

Role play is similar to an in-tray exercise in that it will be based on something that could happen in a day-to-day situation. For example, if the position entails managing difficult people (customers or staff), you may be given a scenario where you have to work through a problem with an actor or member of the assessment team playing the part of a tricky employee/ customer. You will usually be given the scenario beforehand and time to prepare. Don't be surprised if it's filmed as its standard practice enabling the assessors to mark your performance afterwards. It also provides a record in case a candidate challenges their score at a later date and helps with consistency of scoring.

With role-play the assessor will be looking for:

- How you handle difficult situations.

- How you build relationships and rapport with others.

- Whether you take responsibility for what's happening.

- Your problem solving and interpersonal skills.

- How you prepare (if you're given the scenario before the actual role play).

- How you work/behave under pressure.

TOP TIP – Again, consider the **outcome** you want to achieve – this is paramount and where most people fall down. Think about the result you want and write down some key questions/ areas that you need to explore to get to your outcome. If the role play involves an awkward person, one of your questions should be, *"What would you like the outcome to be?"* Then you can explore together where there may be synergies/ areas for compromise between what you both want. You're often looking for a win/win scenario.

WRITTEN REPORTS

Written reports will usually be based on a case study and are intended to test your comprehension, analytical and problem-solving skills. They also give an indication of how good your written English is, as well as your ability to follow instructions.

TOP TIPS - Make sure you stick to time and write a quick outline covering the essential items you want to include. Spend as little time as possible on the draft and start writing your end document as soon as possible. Remember not to waffle, but be concise and succinct. The following is a standard report outline:

1. Introduction

2. Main Body

3. Summary/ Conclusion/ Recommendations.

Alternatively, try thinking outside the box and present the information differently. Unless expressly stated, you don't have to write a full report, consider how you might display the information pictorially in a table or graph for example. Presenting information in an alternative format, while still answering the question, will automatically help you stand out from your competitors.

Put yourself in the assessor's shoes and think about how you would like to see the information presented. The feedback I have from assessors is that they get tired of reading and marking hundreds of reports that are full of waffle and look exactly the same! They give a sigh of relief when someone presents the right information in an alternative way.

Self-Review

A self-review is a written report that is generally completed at the end of an assessment centre. You'll be asked to evaluate your performance, describe what went well, what you could have done better/ differently and what you've learnt. Remember that the assessors are looking for people who can demonstrate the company's competencies, so bear that in mind when you complete your review. They will also want to know how self-aware you are, whether you noticed your mistakes and how you would handle the same problem if it came up again. They will also want to know if you have recognised any development areas.

Unfortunately, again, there's little preparation you can do for this. However, don't be over critical of yourself, be honest giving reasons (where possible) for your actions, together with plans to address development areas.

Meeting With A Manager

The 'meeting with a manager' is different from an interview. It's often positioned at the end of the day providing you with the opportunity to give and receive feedback on the day and to ask any outstanding questions. Again, the manager will be looking for how self-aware you are and if you've picked up on any development areas. It is unusual for this part of the assessment to be marked.

TOP TIPS – ASSESSMENT CENTRES

The following is a list of top tips and common mistakes made by candidates during assessment centres. This information has been collated from the feedback I've received from both assessors, candidates and from my own observations:

1. DON'T JUST DO IT, SHOW THE ASSESSORS YOU'RE DOING IT – If no-one sees or hears you doing or saying something, it can't be marked.

2. MANAGE YOUR TIME – THE top reason people fail during assessment centres is not keeping within the stipulated time limits. If you get invited to an assessment centre, and you don't have a watch (many people now use their phone to tell the time), either borrow one or buy one, it's an investment worth making. You shouldn't rely on your phone for the time as it's unlikely that you'll be allowed to take it into the assessment with you.

3. TACKLE ALL SECTIONS – No matter what the task, try to complete everything in the sequence it's delivered – many candidates miss questions out thinking they'll

go back to them, only to find that they run out of time. If you miss something out, you could lose valuable marks. In an assessment situation, one point can mean the difference between getting the job and not.

4. FOLLOW THE INSTRUCTIONS – Read and follow the instructions carefully. Don't skim read documents as that could mean that you miss important information. Saying the question out loud (if possible) or writing it down often helps people clearly understand what's being asked.

5. DON'T GET SIDE-TRACKED – Remember to stay on track and keep reviewing the question/task at hand so that you don't get distracted. If you don't answer the right question or do something that's not on the agenda, you won't get a score for it, and you'll have wasted valuable time and marks.

6. DON'T PLAN EVERYTHING IN ROUGH – This is especially pertinent when it comes to 'on the day' presentations where you are given the topic and limited time to prepare. You rarely have time to plan everything in draft *and* to re-do it perfectly. Instead, quickly write a rough outline and start working on the end product as soon as possible.

7. DON'T OFFER TO FACILITATE, BE THE TIMEKEEPER OR SCRIBE – It's unlikely that you'll be fully involved in tasks if

you volunteer to take on these responsibilities, potentially handing valuable points to your competitors.

8. PRACTISE, PRACTISE, PRACTISE – I'll keep saying this repeatedly; practise is critical for interview and assessment preparation. Rehearse your interview questions, presentations, online tests, etc. as many times as possible beforehand. It's perfectly acceptable to ask what exercises the assessment centre will consist of. However, if they won't tell you, you can take an educated guess that you will have a competency-based interview and potentially a presentation (usually around what you would hope to achieve in the first ninety days in the role). So be prepared.

9. MAKE SURE THAT YOU KNOW THE COMPETENCIES – You should thoroughly understand the company's competencies, how your skills and experience match them and be able to demonstrate them competently.

10. VISUALISE THINGS GOING WELL – By consistently imagining the day from beginning to end, focussing on your desired outcome in as much detail as possible, you will significantly increase your chances of achieving your desired result.

11. DON'T PANIC! If you didn't do particularly well in one exercise, try not to let it affect the rest of your performance. It's your *overall* score that counts.

CHAPTER 5 - PRESENTATION SKILLS

"Proper preparation prevents presentation predicaments!"

I could write a whole book based purely on presentation skills as it's such a broad topic. I run two-day presentation skills workshops, covering not only how to design and deliver an effective presentation but how to understand the psychology of the audience which enables delegates to deliver their message with impact. While I don't have space go into that amount of detail here, I will give you a solid structure and some top tips which will allow you to prepare and deliver an excellent interview presentation.

Many companies use presentations as a part of their selection process for a range of different jobs. As well as being an integral part of many assessment centres. They are probably the most utilised assessment tool after the interview.

WHEN YOU'RE GIVEN THE TITLE ON THE DAY

If you're required to give a presentation, you will usually be provided with the topic/ title, the timing (duration) and who your audience will be, before the assessment/ interview. However, not always; some companies prefer to give you that information on the day. If that's the case, again, it's important to think about the competencies you will be tested against and have them with you in your folder.

Keep calm and quickly draw up an outline of what you want to cover (don't write down too much information in a draft, as you could run out of time). Think about the key messages that you want to deliver and shape your content as explained in the seven-step structure outlined in this chapter.

Top Tip - THE most frequently used presentation title is based on what you expect to achieve in your first 30/60 or 90 days in the role. Therefore, you're going to be required to do a presentation on the day but don't know the title, give some consideration to how you would answer that question beforehand. Think about what you would want to learn, deliver and achieve in the first few months in the role. There are some excellent books available regarding 'first 90 days' which would be worth investing in.

WHAT MAKES A POOR PRESENTATION

There are nine typical mistakes that people make when preparing and delivering a presentation:

1. Having no clear aim.

2. Not understanding the topic/ what information the assessor wants to see/ hear/ know.

3. Including information that isn't relevant/ important.

4. Not understanding the audience.

5. Using poor visual aids (we've all heard the term or been witness to 'Death by PowerPoint').

6. Not sticking to stipulated time limits.

7. Being dull and uninteresting.

8. Poor delivery - usually a result of inadequate preparation or nerves.

9. Lack of preparation.

PRESENTATION TIMINGS

I have designed an easy to use seven step structure that will help you overcome the common presentation mistakes. But before I tell you about that, it's important to look at how to accurately time your presentation and how much information you should include in each section ('what' to include is covered later).

Taking an example of a ten-minute presentation, here's how you should break it down:

TEN MINUTE PRESENTATION		
Opening *(Two minutes)*	**Content** *(Six minutes - two minutes per key point)*	**Ending** *(Two minutes)*
Tell them what you're going to tell them.	Tell them. *(No more than three key points.)*	Tell them what you've told them.

If you have more than ten minutes, either add additional key points or explain each of the three key points in more detail. Regardless of how much time you have, I would recommend covering a maximum of five points; any

94

more and it will be information overload for your audience and for you!

SEVEN STEP STRUCTURE

1. HAVE A CLEAR AIM

   Make sure you think about and have clear answers to the following questions before you start your preparation:

   - Why are you making the presentation?
   - What is the purpose?
     o To inform?
     o To persuade/sell?
     o To entertain?

   - **What do you want to achieve/what is your desired outcome?** Be clear about your end position. Be SPECIFIC – if you're confused, your audience will be too. What do you want your audience to:
     o Know?
     o Take away?
     o Do differently as a result?

   - What knockout result do you want?

2. KNOW YOUR AUDIENCE

Your audience is likely to be thinking (maybe subconsciously):

"Please tell me something I don't already know."

"Please don't waste my time."

"Please give me something that makes my life easier."

An audience is only interested in the part of your presentation that makes their lives easier; therefore, it's essential to be **relevant, concise and compelling**. **They will also remember what you want them to remember.** The success of your presentation depends on how much what you say coincides with what they want and need to hear.

Consider the following:

- What interests them about the subject?

- What do they already know about it?

- What is their 'stake' in it?

- What 'baggage' might they have about it?

- What issues may be important to them?

- What points may be contentious? (You should avoid being deliberately provocative in an interview situation – you can't afford to have an interviewer turn against you.)

IN SUMMARY:

- What do you want to persuade your audience to do?

- Decide on the result or **outcome** you want to achieve.

- Research your audience:

  o Who are they?

  o What do they *want* to hear/see/feel?

  o What do they *need* to hear/see/feel?

  o What must you tell them to get what YOU want from giving the presentation?

  o What are the audiences starting positions?

3. SELECT THE RIGHT CONTENT

Create a 'statement' that reflects the essence of your presentation which is short, relevant and memorable. Your content must relate back to this, if it doesn't, ditch it. Your statement should encompass:

- What you want the audience to remember above all else.

- What you would say if you only had 10 seconds.

YOUR STATEMENT MUST:

- Be explicitly created for that audience.

- Feel crucial to that audience.

- Stimulate audience thought.

- Be one sentence long.

- Be simple enough to be memorable.

- Should not just state the end position.

Once you have your statement, brainstorm your ideas. There's a great piece of free software that I use for brainstorming and planning content of presentations, workshops and book content. It's useful if you're a visual person and like to see things written down, especially pictorially. The software is called 'Xmind' (xmind.net/).

- Use your 'statement' to brainstorm all the content you could include in your presentation.

- Think about every bit of information available to support your statement, e.g. statistics, anecdotes, stories, facts, testimonials, etc., and list the headings.

- Be inclusive rather than exclusive at this stage – leave the editing until later, just get the ideas down for now.

- Group headings together where appropriate.

ONCE YOU'VE BRAINSTORMED, FILTER THE INFORMATION USING THE FOLLOWING CRITERIA:

- **Must know** – The key points that you want to make and the essential information that supports and illustrates them.

- **Should know** – Desirable information that will help the audience understand the bigger picture. You shouldn't include this in the presentation, but could cover it during a Question and Answer session at the end. You may also wish to put this information in handouts and present them to the audience after your presentation.

- **Could know** - Leave this information out, it's not necessary and will take away from the essential message.

IN SUMMARY:

- Write down, in one sentence, what you want the audience to remember – your statement.

- Brainstorm the information that could flow from the statement.

- Select only the 'must knows' from your brainstorm.

- Put 'should know' information in a handout.

- Leave out the 'could know'.

4. SHAPE THE CONTENT

   Your presentation should have three distinct sections:

   a. INTRODUCTION – *'Tell them what you're going to tell them.'*

      - Open with an attention grabber, which includes your 'statement'. The first few seconds are key, open with:

        o A quote or anecdote.

- A relevant startling statistic.

- A promise.

- A rhetorical question.

- Your first sentence should be striking enough to make your audience listen – your STATEMENT.

- Be risky (but not too risky!) rather than bland.

- Give the audience a jolt, but don't turn them off.

- NEVER start with an apology.

- Tell the audience the purpose of the talk.

- Provide the audience with your presentation plan, i.e. a preview of the main points you intend covering.

b. MAIN BODY - *'Tell them.'*

- Never have no more than five key points, no matter how long your presentation is. If it is ten minutes, then you should use no more than three key points, two minutes each.

- You should illustrate each point with evidence and examples.

c. SUMMARY/ENDING – *'Tell them what you've told them.'*

- End with a strong summary of the purpose and the key points.

- The last two sentences are what people will remember – make sure they're worthy.

- The ending should also be attention-grabbing but not so much that it brings up new questions.

- End with a 'call to action' where possible - something that you want the audience to think or do as a result of your presentation.

- Don't finish with a question or an apology – it would indicate a loss of control.

5. CREATE A SCRIPT

It's essential to have a script to start off with so that you're clear about what you want to say. Once you're comfortable with it and have practised reading it out loud, you can then break it down into bullet point reminders that you can use on the day. **DO NOT use a detailed script for the actual presentation.**

How to write a presentation script:

- Say it out loud as you're writing:

    o It forces you to decide on the best order.

    o It enables you to spot where repetition is necessary and where it's harmful.

    o It helps eliminate clichés and jargon.

    o You can check it against your 'statement.'

    o You'll be able to shape the flow and improve the tone.

- Read it for sense.

- Edit for impact.

- **Use humour** where appropriate.

USING HUMOUR

Humour is an excellent way to get your message across and ensure you make an impact – as long as you make an impact for the *right* reasons:

- TYPES OF HUMOUR TO AVOID:

- o Racism

- o Sexism

- o Impersonations

- o Anything that could be deemed as being unprofessional or discriminatory

- DELIVER HUMOUR:

  - o With precision with confidence

  - o With speed

  - o With practise

IN SUMMARY:

- Write out a baseline script using your structure.

- Edit the text.

- Open with an attention grabber.

- Close with a call to action (where possible) or something memorable.

- **Everything must relate back to your statement**, if it doesn't, ditch it or put it in a handout.

6. DEVELOP VISUAL AIDS

Using visual aids can be tricky. When I refer to visual aids, I mean the presentation software you use (Prezi, PowerPoint, Keynote) as well as props. Nowadays, people are tired of seeing PowerPoint presentations, especially when they are poorly designed or contain too much information, can be a big turn-off for audiences.

If you want to use presentation software that's a bit different, a fantastic alternative to PowerPoint or Apple's Keynote is Prezi, which is available for free, albeit with limited functionality. I now use nothing else for training and presentation purposes, as I find it more engaging. Audiences tend to pay more attention to it because it provides the ability to present information in a different format which is generally more appealing.

TOP TIPS FOR USING VISUAL AIDS

When creating visual aids such as presentations in Prezi, PowerPoint, or Keynote you should bear the following points in mind:

- Only use them to *support* what you're saying.

- They should be a secondary focus; they shouldn't contain the whole presentation or your entire script.

- Use them sparingly – for maximum impact have minimum slides.

- Use them to express, explain or describe.

- They should reinforce the main messages.

- Slides should be simple, bright and have plenty of white space.

- Pictures and graphics always beat text, especially for the 'visual' audience members.

- Avoid too much animation as its distracting.

- Keep text size and font consistent on each slide (attention to detail is critical).

- Avoid graphs/ tables containing too much information.

- Prepare a backup document (just in case there's a problem with the IT).

USING PROPS

- Use 'accessories,' e.g. videos, sound bites, product examples, music, etc. where appropriate to support your presentation. Such accessories are perfect for getting your message across to visual and kinesthetic audience members (I discuss different communications styles later in this chapter).

- Keep props out of sight until they're needed as they can distract the audience. If you leave them in view throughout your presentation, the audience will be wondering what they're for rather than listening to you.

- Remove props once you've finished with them to lessen the distraction.

NOTE - YOU DON'T HAVE TO USE AN ON-SCREEN PRESENTATION! We are so used to using presentation software that it may not occur to you that you don't have to. If you're confident enough, you can just talk or use a flip chart to illustrate your key points. If you decide to do this, my only concern would be how you come across to your 'visual' audience members who respond to visual styles of communication.

7. PREPARE YOUR NOTES

When it comes to making notes for use during your presentation, there are some critical 'do's' and 'don'ts':

- DON'T USE A DETAILED SCRIPT - If you try to use extensive notes, it's likely that you'll lose your place and become flustered. Prepare bulleted notes by distilling relevant key points from your full script onto small index cards. Make sure you number the cards and find some way of attaching them together in sequence. That way, if you drop them (which I've seen particularly nervous presenters do), you won't lose your place.

- DON'T USE SHORTHAND – When you're under pressure, it's likely that you won't be able to remember the meaning of something that you've written in shorthand.

- DO TYPE OR WRITE YOUR NOTES IN A LARGE FONT – Also use adequate spacing between each line, this will make them easier to read under pressure. Some people like to transfer their presentation notes to an iPad/tablet; be careful if you do that, as you can quickly lose your place or swipe to the wrong page. Also, ensure that your tablet is fully charged.

- YOUR NOTES SHOULD ONLY BE THERE AS A PROMPT - When I'm training or giving a presentation, I rarely use notes. I know what I want to say and use the key points on the screen as my prompts to remind me of the order rather than detailing everything I should be saying.

- DON'T PUT ALL YOUR CONTENT ON SLIDES AND READ IT OUT – If you do this, your presentation will not flow, and the audience will try to read your slides rather than listening to what you're saying. If you do this, you will undoubtedly score low marks. This is where the phrase, 'Death by PowerPoint' comes from.

TOP TIPS - PRESENTING WITH IMPACT

1. PRACTISE

- **Rehearse your presentation as many times as possible** both for real and through clear visualisation.

- Check content and timings.

- Check that visual aids and props are working.

2. CONTROL YOUR BREATHING

- Learn to breathe deeply and in a controlled manner - Use the breathing exercise from the next chapter to help you.

- Controlling your breathing helps control nerves and makes it easier for others to understand you.

3. BE AWARE OF YOUR MANNERISMS

- We communicate nerves through our mannerisms.

- Identify what gives your nerves away.

- If you know that you use fillers repeatedly such as *"erm" "like"* or *"you know"* etc., practise taking a breath rather than saying the word. If you actively change those unwanted words for something else or take a breath instead, with consistent practise, you'll eradicate them from your vocabulary altogether.

- An excellent way to recognise your unhelpful mannerisms is to video yourself giving your presentation. If you notice something you don't like, make a conscious effort to change it and practise the new way as many times as possible.

4. DEVELOP A POSITIVE ATTITUDE

- Be aware of your negative 'internal talk.'

- Negative self-talk can inhibit high-performance. Remember, *'Thoughts Become Things'* and *'we get what we think about'.* Therefore, visualise yourself giving your presentation and everything going perfectly.

5. VISUALISE

'The mind can't tell the difference between something that's vividly imagined and something real.'

- Practise visualising the whole presentation going perfectly. Create a video in your mind, see what you'd see, hear what you'd hear and feel what you'd feel in as much detail as possible. Make it big, bright and noisy and run that video as many times as you possibly can before the big day, as well as just before you present, if possible.

- Practise is THE best way to halt nerves. Whether you do it for real or just in your mind, it has the same effect on your nervous system.

- Use fear as a cattle prod for preparation.

6. USE POSITIVE BODY LANGUAGE TO BUILD RAPPORT.

- Smile.

- Stand straight.

- Maintain eye contact by scanning the audience, looking them in the eye as you do.

- Use positive facial expressions.

- Be open and assertive. Keep your palms on view and use open hand gestures. Hiding your palms, tells others (subconsciously) that you have something to hide.

- Be aware of habits/mannerisms.

- Don't pace; it's distracting.

- Don't stare at one person; you'll make them feel uncomfortable.

- Don't look over people's heads; it freaks audiences out when presenters do that. It makes them wonder what you're looking at towards the back of the room. Some coaches teach presenters to do that, but it really goes against what I recommend. It does not help you create rapport with your audience; they will spend more time wondering what you're looking at towards the back of the room than listening to what you have to say.

7. CONTROL YOUR VOICE

- PROJECT YOUR VOICE WITHOUT SHOUTING – You should practise this at home if you're not used to it.

- SPEAK SLOWLY – We tend to speak more quickly when we're nervous. Make a conscious effort to slow down your speech.

- VARY TONE, VOLUME, AND SPEED – Try to inject as much life into your voice as possible keeping delegates thoroughly engaged.

- PRONOUNCE WORDS DISTINCTLY – Don't mumble, you want people to hear and understand what you're saying.

- USE PAUSES – Often pausing in the right place can be quite dramatic. Pause where you want the audience to think about what you've just stated.

Other Top Presentation Tips

1. LET THE ROOM SETTLE DOWN – Wait until the audience is ready to listen before you start, ensuring that you have everyone's attention.

2. REHEARSE SAYING YOUR FIRST LINE OUT LOUD – Your first line sets the tone for the rest of the presentation. Focus on cutting out the fillers such as *"OK," "so," "right"*. If you get your opening statement right, it sets the tone for the rest of the presentation.

3. BE RECEPTIVE AND OBSERVE YOUR AUDIENCE'S BODY LANGUAGE – I am acutely aware of my audience at all times, and if I feel that they may be drifting (I can tell that by watching their body language, facial expressions and where they rest their eyes), I'll do something unexpected. For example, I'll get them to stand up, or I'll vary the tone of my voice or ask an unexpected question. All these techniques draw the audience's attention back to what I'm saying as it interrupts their current thinking pattern.

4. NAIL YOUR ENDING - Your conclusion is critical; it's what the audience will go away remembering the most. Therefore, make sure that you end on a high rather than letting your presentation fizzle out.

5. STICK TO TIMINGS – It's vital that you stick to your schedule. Be aware that even though you may have practised your presentation at home, it's likely, unless you are really strict with yourself, that you'll go over the allotted time. That's because, for some reason, candidates often add things that weren't in their original script during their 'live' delivery. They'll often misinterpret a facial expression and feel they have to justify what they've just said, adding additional content. Stick to what you've prepared as much as possible. Otherwise, you will go over, and you'll be stopped, potentially without having had time to get all your critical points across.

6. PRACTISE MAKES PERFECT – I can't emphasise this enough. Good quality rehearsal will make a massive difference to your performance on the day.

ANSWERING AUDIENCE QUESTIONS

Questions are an inevitable part of presentations and something many of my clients fear the most. Here are my guidelines for successfully managing this section of your presentation:

- If you have limited time (most interview presentations are time sensitive) tell the audience before you start, that you'll be taking questions at the end. If you do get asked a question mid-flow, don't stop to answer, say, "I'll answer that at the end if that's OK?"

- If you get asked a question that you don't know the answer to, don't panic. Say that you'll look into it and provide answers after the interview. I usually say something like, *"Oh good question. Leave it with me, and I'll get back to you before the end of the day."* Most people will be happy with that.

- If your presentation isn't subject to strict timings, ask if the audience has any questions *before* you give your summary/ ending. That way, if you get asked a tricky question, you aren't going to end on a potential negative.

- Always pause before you reply to give yourself some breathing space. This can help stop you from saying the wrong thing.

- Never patronise, e.g. *"I'm glad you asked that..."*

- If you don't know the answer, be honest and say so. You can't be expected to know everything.

- If a question isn't relevant or is only applicable to that person, don't be afraid to interrupt and tell them that you'll be happy to answer after the presentation.

- If you're unsure what someone means, ask them for clarification.

- Keep answers brief.

- **Never get defensive.** If you get asked a question and become defensive, it can harm the audience's perception of you. If you feel yourself getting defensive, take a deep breath before answering and consciously *choose* how you reply.

- Beware of getting into too much dialogue and spending too much time answering one question. Take it offline if possible, I usually say something like, *"Do you mind if we pick this up afterwards?"*

- Prepare for difficult question beforehand by writing down what you could be asked and how you would answer. Here are some examples:

  o What is the most embarrassing/ challenging/ appalling question I could be asked?

  o What would I ask if I were deeply cynical?

  o What would I ask if someone else giving the same presentation?

  o What question could expose my greatest weakness?

o   What questions would I love the audience to ask?

- Use the three 'S's' – **SAY IT. SUPPORT IT. SHUT IT!** Avoid waffling.

PRESENTATION SKILLS SUMMARY

1. **Practise, Practise, Practise!** The more you practise, the better you'll become. Public speaking is a set of skills that can be learnt.

2. Have no more than three critical points in a ten-minute presentation – no more than five points if you have longer.

3. *"Tell them what you're going to tell them, tell them and then tell them what you've told them."*

4. Use small prompt cards NOT a detailed script – remember to number the cards and fix them together so that if you drop them, you can easily find your place.

5. If you use presentation software, e.g. Prezi/ PowerPoint/ Keynote, have plenty of 'white space' on the screen and make sure you test that everything is working correctly. Avoid putting your whole presentation on the screen. It's distracting, and

people will spend more time reading what you've written rather than listening to you.

6. Always have a backup handout just in case your IT fails on the day. Unfortunately, it's common for there to be problems with laptops, projectors and TVs, etc. Therefore, having a backup is always important.

7. Prepare for any possible questions.

8. Use positive, open body language.

9. Stay on time – practise will help you with that. When I have to stick to time, and there isn't a clock in the room, I take my watch off and put it somewhere so that it can be seen easily without drawing attention to the fact that I'm looking at it.

10. Have a glass of water on hand – we often get dry mouth when we're nervous.

11. Remember that you know your content; your audience doesn't. Therefore, if you make a mistake, don't admit it, move on – it's unlikely that the audience will notice unless you tell them!

12. Video yourself giving your presentation, that way you'll be able to see what works and what doesn't. You'll also notice if you have any unhelpful mannerisms which you need to address.

13. Visualise your perfect outcome. By frequently imagining a positive result, you'll adequately prepare yourself for the real thing.

Chapter 6 – On The Day

"If you never try, you'll never know."

There are some basic 'dos' and 'don'ts' regarding how to conduct yourself before, during and after an interview. You may think that some of the items I've listed in this chapter are a bit basic; however, if it's in here, it means that it's a common mistake regularly made by candidates.

Personal Presentation

Dress to impress – never underestimate how important your appearance is when it comes to interviews. How you present yourself speaks volumes about you. It's an excellent indicator of how conscientious and professional you are. It gives the interviewer a good idea of your values and personal standards, which they will assume you will apply to everything you do. For example, if you're sloppily dressed, it could be presumed that you will be slapdash in your work. Alternatively, if you pay attention to what you are wearing and look neat and tidy, then it will almost be taken for granted that you will apply those values to your job.

During my research, I spoke to many recruiters who said that they wouldn't employ somebody who wasn't appropriately dressed. I've also had 'visual' interviewers say that they have rejected people if their shoes aren't polished or if their heels are down-trodden. Others stated that if the interviewee's clothes were mismatched or un-ironed, that would be enough of a reason for rejection, even if they gave an excellent interview! Therefore, don't underestimate the importance of your personal presentation.

I do have a caveat here, the 'dress' advice I'm providing in this chapter is for regular jobs such as office/ management/ shop floor/ warehouse, etc. were expected interview dress is fairly standard. However, if you are applying for a design role, e.g. fashion designer, buyer, etc., there may be a little more 'give' regarding artistic freedom. Certain types of companies may also be more flexible in their dress code, preferring candidates who have a bit more individuality or who are more casual. My advice would be to find out the company's uniform/dress code beforehand. However, if in doubt, follow the guidance below.

PERSONAL PRESENTATION - MEN

- WEAR A SUIT – I used to say that you must ALWAYS wear a suit with a shirt and tie for interviews. However, many companies are now moving away from suits (especially ties) to more relaxed attire. Some even include their dress policy in the interview invitation letter/email. If they do this, you should always adhere to their dress policy. If they go to the trouble of indicating their dress code and you ignore it, there's a strong possibility that you will be rejected.

   However, if you're in doubt, no matter what role you're applying for, whether it is office based or otherwise, I recommend wearing a suit. If you don't own one, buy one, it's probably one of the best investments you could make. If you spend £100 on a suit, and you land a job that pays you £1000s then that £100 was a great investment. If you borrow one, make sure that it's reasonably current and fits. If it's an old suit, it can give the impression that you are out of date. Also, ill-fitting clothes will not give you the desired effect, i.e. that you are smart and well presented.

   There is always a lot of debate about tie wearing during my career management workshops, and when I canvassed opinion during my research for this book, there were very mixed reactions. Some thought it a good idea, others' not so much. Again, if you aren't comfortable wearing a tie, or aren't used to it, I suggest that you do your research on the company's dress code. If in doubt, wear the tie (after all, you can always take it off when you get there if you think it's not appropriate).

- The suit should be a dark colour, and the shirt and tie should match but shouldn't be too bright.

- Make sure your clothes are pressed, with no visible creases - that includes the back of your shirt just in case you need to remove your jacket. When I interview candidates in warm offices, I'll often ask if they want to take off their jackets – I've had a couple tell me they can't because they only ironed the front of their shirt!

- Avoid wearing cartoon/novelty ties or socks – socks should be dark and match your suit, ties should match your outfit and shirt. Many people think it makes them look like they have a personality by wearing novelty items; on the contrary, it makes you appear silly and immature.

- Your shoes should be dark and polished – heels shouldn't be 'down-trodden'. No sandals, ever!

- Keep jewellery to a minimum (remove any earrings and piercings) and keep tattoos covered, especially if the role is office based.

- Make sure your hair is clean and neat and that you've recently shaved or, if you have a beard, that it's manicured.

- Keep aftershave light – you don't want to overpower the interviewer, that's a major turnoff.

- Your nails should be short, neat and clean.

PERSONAL PRESENTATION - WOMEN

- I recommend that women also wear a suit, despite there being a downturn in their popularity in recent years. Whether you choose a dress, skirt or trouser suit, it should be smart and professional, preferably in darker colours. Avoid wearing bright and pastel colours for interviews and make sure that everything is matching. Again, you can pick up a professional looking suit for under £100, and it's a great investment if it helps you get your next role. You'll also feel more confident if you are well presented.

- If you really don't want to wear a suit, you must NOT wear knitwear - knitwear is not smart enough and far too casual for an interview. Instead, wear a tailored dress or trousers/ skirt and a stylish shirt or blouse.

- Ensure your clothes are clean and well pressed. Un-ironed garments are not acceptable and will make you look sloppy and unprofessional.

- Wearing light makeup, (even if you don't usually wear it) is a good idea; even just using mascara and lip gloss will make you look more polished. On the other hand, don't overdo it; leave the heavy makeup, false lashes, and bright lipstick for the weekend, as it is distracting for many employers.

- Keep your nails neat and tidy, you don't have to have a manicure, but it's great if you do. No chipped polish please and keep nail art to a minimum; you want the interviewers to be focused on you, not on your nails. Well-manicured nails, again, indicate that you are detail conscious and have high personal standards.

- Less is more when it comes to jewellery – no big hoop earrings and statement necklaces. If you wear a long chain, make sure that you don't fidget with it during the interview as that can be distracting.

- Style your hair so that it looks neat and well groomed. An 'evening up-do' isn't appropriate for an interview.

- Your shoes should be dark in colour and polished. **No sandals allowed, not even in summer**. You should wear full shoes or boots only (boots should only be worn in winter). Make sure the heels are not worn down.

- Your perfume shouldn't be overpowering. There's nothing worse for an interviewer than having to sit in a room with someone wearing strong scent. Not only is it uncomfortable for the recruiter, but it's unpleasant for following candidates to have to smell someone else's lingering scent.

- Keep tattoos covered, especially if the role is office based and remove any visible piercings (stud earrings are fine).

If you're meeting with a recruitment consultant, you don't necessarily have to wear a full suit (and tie), but as I've mentioned in Book 2 in of the Your Dream Job series, 'Finding Your Dream Job', you should NEVER wear jeans. You must always look professional, and I would still recommend that you wear a suit.

Before The Interview

1. Arrive on time

- You should NEVER be late. If you can't be on time for an interview, it's a pretty good indicator of your reliability.

- If you are late, don't make up a false excuse as it's likely that the interviewer will check your story. If someone is late for an interview, I will always investigate to see if their reason is correct. I'll look to see if there are hold-ups on the roads, or review trains schedules to see if they're running on time, etc. so don't assume that other interviewers won't do the same.

- If there is an unavoidable holdup, inform the recruiter as soon as possible. The sooner you tell them, the better it will be for you.

- Do a trial run of getting to the venue preferably **at the same time and day as your interview**. I had one client who ignored this advice and did his trial run into Manchester City Centre on a Sunday afternoon - his meeting was scheduled for 9.00 am on Monday morning. He turned up over an hour late on the day because he hadn't taken rush hour into consideration when planning his journey.

- Always aim to arrive at least 15 minutes early. If you give yourself a bit of extra time, you won't feel rushed or panicked, and you'll have a chance to calm down, collect your thoughts, take some deep breaths and do your visualisation exercises before your interview starts.

- You may also want to confirm if there's parking and if the company will reserve you a space. This is an issue I often come across when visiting clients. If I don't ask about parking spaces, sometimes one won't have been arranged, and I'll end up in a residential parking area, where it's illegal to park.

2. BE NICE TO THE RECEPTIONIST (and everyone else you meet!)

If I'm interviewing, I will *always* ask the receptionist how the candidate interacted with them. The way candidates treat the receptionist or the person sent to greet them (if it's not an interviewer) is a good indicator of their personality and values.

I'll always remember a director I was managing a recruitment programme with, coming into a pre-interview meeting outraged. Someone had cut him up in the car park, taken a space he was patiently waiting for, and when he challenged the perpetrator, he was greeted with a tirade of verbal abuse and unacceptable gesturing. It took quite a while and a strong cup of coffee to calm him down. When the candidate walked in the room, can you guess who it was? Yep, the angry man from the car park. Not surprisingly, he didn't get the job!

3. TURN OFF YOUR PHONE

Turn your phone off as soon as you arrive at the building, this is such simple advice, yet so important, and something many candidates forget to do. Not only is it unprofessional, but it could put you off track if your phone rings when you're in mid-flow. It's also very annoying for the interviewer. If you do forget and it does ring, DO NOT ANSWER IT! Apologise to the interviewer and turn it off immediately.

The same advice is applicable if you're meeting a recruitment consultant. TURN YOUR PHONE OFF. Don't leave it on the table and check it during the meeting if you see a message come through! You'd be surprised how many people do that according to recruitment consultant colleagues - it's unprofessional and rude.

4. BE POSITIVE

If the interviewer asks you how you are, or how your journey was, don't complain. Simply say something like, *"Great thanks."* One recruiter was recently telling me that when she asked that question, a candidate replied, *"Well I'm a bit tired and stressed, to be honest."* No recruiter wants to hear that. Be upbeat and positive, even if you aren't feeling it.

5. WATCH YOUR BODY LANGUAGE

Smile, make eye contact use a firm, *dry* handshake. Nobody likes someone who can't look them in the eye; it's creepy. Even though you may be nervous, it's important to smile and make good eye contact with everyone in the room.

Also, use a good firm, dry handshake. Many women (and some men) don't know how to shake hands properly and have developed a light, limp handshake. Non-verbally that says that you are unsure about yourself and your abilities. Many people also consider a light handshake to indicate a lack of strength of character. Therefore, if you know that you don't have a firm handshake, or you feel uncomfortable shaking hands, practise it.

On the reverse, no-one wants to have their hand crushed. It is particularly off-putting when a man squeezes a woman's hand too tightly; leaving her hand in pain where her rings have marked her fingers (I'm speaking from experience here!). It shouldn't be a show of strength.

If, for religious reasons, you are unable to shake hands, politely explain why. Not everyone will be aware it can be contrary to some religions' etiquette.

During The Interview

There are some critical do's and don'ts during the interview. It's often the small things that make the most significant impact.

The following are my top tips:

1. WAIT TO BE ASKED TO SIT DOWN - It's polite to wait to be invited.

2. SIT STILL AND COMFORTABLY AND USE POSITIVE BODY LANGUAGE (see the next section for more information on body language) - Sit back in your chair as soon as you sit down, if you 'perch' on the end, there's nowhere for you to go and it's likely that you'll end up feeling uncomfortable.

3. DON'T CHEW GUM – This seems obvious, but you'd be surprised how many people do it. It's incredibly unprofessional and very off-putting for a recruiter. I remember a client who was perfect for a role; however, the recruiter rejected him because he chewed gum throughout the interview. The interviewer was horrified when he was relaying this to me. When I asked my client, what possessed him to chew gum, he said that when he gets nervous, his mouth can dry up, and he thought chewing gum would alleviate the problem

4. IF YOU'RE OFFERED A DRINK, ALWAYS TAKE IT – If asked whether you would like tea, coffee or water, I suggest accepting water. When we feel under pressure, our mouths tend to dry up and, therefore, having some water on hand would be helpful. If you know you suffer from dry mouth, take a bottle of water in with you. However, don't draw the water through the bottle top as it makes an awful noise. Instead, remove the lid or ask the interviewer for a glass.

5. DON'T MAKE COPIOUS NOTES – It's okay to write the occasional point down. However, you can't possibly concentrate on what the interviewer is asking while you're busy writing. Incidentally, I find it very distracting if a candidate makes lots of notes, it's not

necessary and contrary to popular belief, it doesn't make you look more professional.

6. DON'T APOLOGISE FOR BEING NERVOUS – It sets the wrong tone for the interview. Make sure that you do your preparation, breathing exercises and Superman stance (explained later in this chapter) before the interview to help to control any nerves.

7. DON'T FIDGET - If you're aware that you're prone to fidgeting with your hair/ pen/ necklace etc., remove temptation. It can be very distracting for a recruiter if someone's continually clicking a pen or fiddling with a chain or security pass.

8. DON'T FLIRT OR CURSE - I find it amazing that I have to include this point. However, it's happened to me a few times over the years. People have attempted to flirt with me or have used inappropriate language during an interview. Both are unacceptable and are likely to result in your rejection, no matter how good the rest of your performance is.

9. MAKE EYE CONTACT WITH EVERYONE IN THE ROOM – Don't just address your answers to the person who asked you the question; share your gaze between everyone in the room. If you stare at one person for too long, it can make them feel uncomfortable. If

there's a note-taker, look at them also. Just because they have their head down doesn't mean that they can't sense your gaze.

10. NEVER UNDERESTIMATE THE NOTE-TAKER – I was once interviewing with two directors to fill a board director vacancy. I was taking the interview notes for no other reason than the fact that I'm good at it (after many years' worth of practice). During the interview, I asked a few questions, and the interviewee (a man) proceeded to direct his answers to the other two (male) directors, completely ignoring me. All I can assume is that he thought that because I was a woman, I was only there in a note-taking capacity (despite the fact he had been told my role at the beginning of the interview). Do you think he got the job? Absolutely not! We took his behaviour to indicate that he was both sexist and overly status-conscious; neither of which were acceptable traits within our organisation.

11. DON'T BE OVERLY CONFIDENT (ARROGANT) - Nobody likes arrogance, and there's a fine line between that and confidence.

12. DON'T GET TOO PERSONAL OR FAMILIAR – This can be a problem when you know one or more of the interviewers; it can become uncomfortable for them

if you are too personal. It's also crucial to still give full answers using the STAR format, especially in a competency-based interview. I've known candidates fail because they assumed that the interviewer knew what they'd done, and mistakenly thought that they didn't need to explain themselves. In a competency-based interview, if you don't say it, they can't mark it. Knowing the interviewer is irrelevant.

Alternatively, if you're the type of person who builds rapport quickly, and you find yourself in synergy with one/all of your interviewers, don't get lulled into a false sense of security and let your guard down. Also, don't shorten names or be too personal. Remain professional at all times.

13. TELL THE TRUTH; LIES WILL BE FOUND OUT – When I once interviewed a candidate who unbeknown to me, had lied on his CV and continued to lie about his skills and achievements during the interview. I offered him the job because I had no reason to believe that he wasn't truthful. Not long after he started, it became apparent that he didn't have the skills or the experience necessary for the role and subsequently he was dismissed during his probationary period.

I've witnessed an unusual phenomenon when it comes to interviews; people will say absolutely anything to get a role - even if they don't want it, or they don't have the skills to be able to do it! Please don't do this, as you will harm yourself and your credibility in the long run if you get the job and can't do it.

14. SPEAK IN ONLY FAVOURABLE TERMS ABOUT YOUR CURRENT ROLE AND EMPLOYER ~ Do not be disrespectful or complain about your current employer, no matter how disgruntled you are or how badly you think you've been treated. No company will employ you if you do. It's unprofessional, and it will make you look like a complainer/ troublemaker.

To illustrate this point; during interview preparation with a client, I explained to her the importance of only saying constructive/ positive things about her previous employer. I was concerned about how she may come across as she had been made redundant and was feeling particularly disgruntled about her perceived mistreatment by the company.

She called me after an interview and said, *"I think I've blown it. I launched into how horrible the redundancy process was and what I really thought about the company and how they treated me."* She was right; she had blown it. She didn't get the job even though she thought she'd done well with everything else. When she called the company for feedback (something I urge all my clients to do), they confirmed that she failed because of her attitude.

15. DON'T 'BLAG' OR BLUFF YOUR WAY THROUGH – Interviewers are rarely looking for the finished article. If you don't know how to do something, tell the truth but explain how you would go about addressing the development area or finding out the information.

16. AVOID USING 'WE' – Overusing the word 'we' e.g. *"we arranged"*, *"we provided,"* *"we delivered"* can lead an interviewer to believe that you can only achieve results as part of a team or worse, that you were lying about your personal achievements on your CV.

17. REMEMBER TO BREATHE AND BE POSITIVE! I'd also add that you should be enthusiastic as it's easy to interpret a lack of passion for lack of interest.

18. REMEMBER TO SMILE - When we smile, it not only helps us feel better by releasing endorphins (the feel-good hormone) into the bloodstream, but it also produces an automatic smile response in others, making them feel better too.

19. THE INTERVIEW ISN'T OVER UNTIL YOU'VE LEFT THE PREMISES – Wait to make any phone calls until you're out of earshot, you never know who's listening/ watching.

Wait until you're in your car or well away from the building. Also, be careful what you say to the person who walks you out of the building. Be under no illusion that everything you say and do will be under scrutiny from the moment you arrive until the moment you leave the building (and car park!).

COMMUNICATION SKILLS & RAPPORT BUILDING

Your overall communication skills are critical throughout the assessment process; however, I want first to concentrate on your physiology. Physiology encompasses your body language, facial expressions and paralinguistics, i.e. *how* we say things (our pitch/tone, etc.).

The most significant part of how we communicate is not through the words we use, but through our physiology and paralinguistics which are mainly driven by our subconscious. Figure 2 shows the percentage difference between how the words we use, our body language and paralinguistics contribute towards our overall communication.

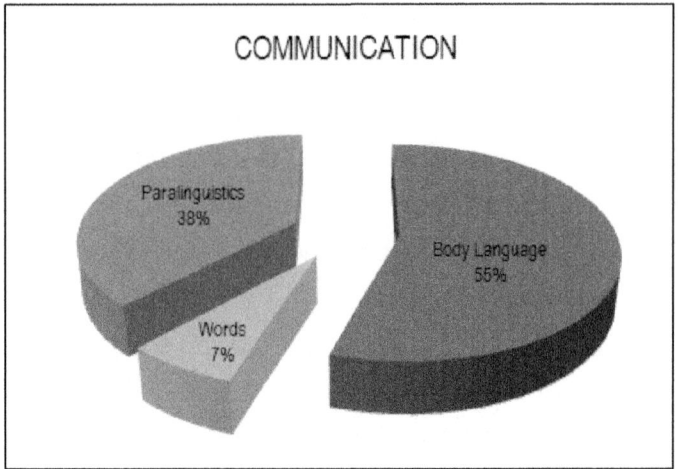

COMMUNICATION

FIGURE 2

As you can see, words are only 7% of what we 'say'. Therefore, it's essential that what we communicate through our body language, facial expressions, tone, speed and pitch of our voices is consistent with our words; they must be congruent.

To do this, you should use positive physiology:

1. Avoid crossing your arms, even if you're cold, as it indicates that you are closed, uncomfortable, and an interviewer could perceive you as being hostile.

2. Don't put your hands behind your head. That suggests arrogance.

3. Crossed legs are fine; however, your feet should be pointing towards the interviewer(s). Whether you're sitting or standing, where you position your feet is a good indicator of where you subconsciously want to go; if they are pointing towards the door, then that's a giveaway as to where you'd rather be, i.e. out of the door!

4. Keep your hands on your lap and use open-palmed gestures. Open palms signify that you have nothing to hide and is where the term, 'showing your hand' originates. If you conceal your palms/hands, the other person will subconsciously think that you have something to hide.

5. Sit up straight in your chair and s slightly forward, which indicates that you're interested and attentive. Leaning backwards communicates that you don't want to be there, you don't like what's being said, and potentially, that you're uncomfortable or possibly even arrogant, especially if you 'rock' back in your chair.

   I once interviewed a candidate who was so laid back that he was almost horizontal the way he was sitting. That gave me the impression that he wasn't interested, that he thought himself too good for us and didn't care whether he got the job or not.

6.   Smile and nod in agreement in the right places so that the interviewer can see that you're fully engaged.

7.   Pay attention to the pace/ speed and tone of your voice. When we're nervous, we tend to talk more quickly and at a slightly higher pitch (men and women). Therefore, consciously slow your speech down – I suggest you try this when you practise your STAR examples or presentation. If in doubt, a top tip is to mimic the tonality and pace of the interviewer. By doing that, you'll also be building excellent subconscious rapport with them.

8.   Don't talk over the interviewer as it can be irritating. Wait until they've finished speaking before you reply. I know that can be hard to do when you're keen to get your point across and to show that you're in agreement. However, it can be very frustrating for the other person, and if you don't hear the full question or statement, you may say something inappropriate or that's not pertinent.

9.   Subtly mirror the body language of the primary interviewer.   By doing that, again you'll be subconsciously creating excellent rapport.

There's a section in my book *'Thoughts Become Things'* available on Amazon, regarding how to build rapport using your physiology, which is an essential influencing technique.

COMMUNICATION STYLES

We communicate in four styles; through what we see, hear, feel and think. Although we do use all four, we tend to have a preference, especially in stressful situations. Primarily, our subconscious drives our communication, and, therefore, it may not even occur to you that another person's style differs from yours. Unless someone has the same style as you, it can mean that you are speaking different languages.

In an interview situation, it's vital that we cover all four styles.

Visual - See	👁
Auditory - Hear	👂
Kinesthetic - Feel	🏃
Auditory Digital - Think	🧠

VISUAL

People with a visual preference will want to *see* that you've prepared, they:

- Learn by 'seeing.'

- Judge/ make decisions based on what they see.

- Are organised, neat, well-groomed and like to see the same in others.

- Visualise and are imaginative

- Speak faster than other styles

- Make lots of notes

- Like face to face interaction

- Like the bigger picture rather than detail

- Like to 'see' evidence

To appeal to a visual interviewer:

- Make sure you present a polished appearance. Dress smartly, paying attention to detail, e.g. polished shoes and well-pressed clothes.

- Take a folder with you containing the information discussed above and evidence of what you've achieved (where appropriate).

People with an auditory preference will want to *hear* that what you've done and how your skills, experience and achievements fit their requirements. They:

- Learn by listening and asking questions.

- Judge/ make decisions based on what they hear.

- Like to hear how to do something.

- Prefer bigger picture to detail.

- Make few notes, if any.

- Remember what you say.

- Like to hear that you're passionate about what you do.

- Want to hear that you have the skills and experience.

To appeal to an auditory interviewer:

- Using paralinguistics is essential, pitch, tone, pace of your speech. A top tip is to mirror the interviewers.

- Practise talking about your CV and achievements using the STAR format. You can even use 'Situation', 'Task', 'Action', 'Result' within your answer, e.g.:

  - *"The situation was..."*

  - *"The task was..."*

  - *"The actions I took were..."*

  - *"The results were..."*

Not only will it appeal to an auditory interviewer, but it will help you stay on track with your answer and minimise waffling.

KINESTHETIC

People with a kinesthetic preference will want to *feel* that you want the job and are passionate about what you do. They:

- Learn by 'doing' – having a go.

- Judge/make decisions based on gut feeling/ intuition.

- Are generally more sensitive than other styles, and dress more for comfort.

- Tend to be real 'people, people'.

- Can be introspective, may not ask too many questions.

- Tend to be 'Touchy Feely' - stand closer to others,

- and body language to show that you are passionate about what you do.

To appeal to a Kinesthetic interviewer:

- Make sure you use your paralinguistics.

- Use a firm, dry handshake.

- Make sure you give eye contact to all of the interviewers.

AUDITORY DIGITAL

People with an Auditory Digital preference want details; facts and figures. If you are vague and only give the big picture, that will trouble someone with an AD style. They:

- Like to analyse data.

- Judge/make decisions based on data and facts.

- Enjoy problem-solving.

- Detail conscious.

- Tend to be quieter - less animated (voice and body).

- Prefer structure and sequence (using the STAR format will help with that).

- Will want to know that you have facts to back up your answers.

To appeal to an Auditory Digital interviewer:

- Know your facts and figures – they will not be impressed if you are vague. Be prepared for them to quiz you on detail.

- Don't waffle and keep to the point – they like sequence, so answer questions using the STAR format, e.g. 'The situation was.... The task was....', etc.

SUMMARY OF COMMUNICATION STYLES

VISUAL	• Make decisions based on what they see • Ensure your appearance is neat and you're well groomed • Take a smart, professional looking folder with you to show you've prepared
AUDITORY	• Make decisions based on what they hear • Use the STAR format to explain your achievements adequately

	• They respond well to paralinguistics – monotone bores them
KINESTHETIC	• Make decisions based on gut feeling/intuition • They want to feel that you want the job, you have the skills and passion! • Use appropriate body language - make eye contact/be open
AUDITORY DIGITAL	• Make decisions based on facts • Know your numbers and give details • They like sequence, use the STAR format

WHAT TO TAKE INTO AN INTERVIEW

You should always take a professional looking folder with you. You can get them quite cheaply from stationers or even the stationery section at large supermarkets. The faux leather style that is open on three sides is perfect, or if you want to splash out, a genuine leather one, I'd advise the latter for senior management positions. DO NOT use a tatty old looking paper folder or regular notepad with your notes clumsily stuffed inside; that won't impress anyone.

Why should you use a professional looking folder? For the 'visual' interviewer - I'm a visual person, therefore, if someone turns up at an interview without outwardly 'showing' me that they've prepared, I won't be impressed; I'll actually assume that they haven't done any preparation.

If you're an auditory (hearing) or kinesthetic (feeling) person, it may never occur to you to do this, but it's important because you don't know which of the preferences your interviewer(s) will have. It's one of the small things that can make a big difference.

Your folder should contain:

1. TWO COPIES OF YOUR CV – You *must* take your CV with you especially if you either completed an application form when applied for the role or if you got the interview through a recruitment consultant. If you completed an application form, then it's beneficial to let the recruiter see how good your CV is.

    If you applied through a recruitment consultant, it's likely that will have re-designed your CV in their standard format which may not do you justice. Also, there have been times when I've gone for interviews, and the interviewer has forgotten to bring a copy of my CV with them. Having your own copies shows that you prepare and anticipate future needs.

2. YOUR ACHIEVEMENTS IN THE STAR FORMAT – Take the bulleted examples of your achievements with two on each sheet of A4 or each one on separate individual cards, with the associated competency clearly written at the top of each.

3. YOUR (TYPED) QUESTIONS FOR THE INTERVIEWER.

4. A COPY OF THE COMPANY'S COMPETENCIES (if applicable) – You should include this especially if you're going to an assessment centre. If you're allowed to have it with you, then you should refer to it throughout the day to ensure that you stay on track.

5. COPIES OF SIGNIFICANT INFORMATION FROM THE RECRUITER'S WEBSITE OR FROM YOUR RESEARCH – I recently had a meeting with a prospective client (I prepare for such meetings in much the same way as I would for an interview). During my research on their website, I came across an interesting document that I thought may be useful. I printed off a copy and put it in my folder intending to ask them about it if there was time. During the meeting, I was making notes, and the client saw the copy of their document in my folder and was impressed that I'd gone to the trouble of printing it.

6. COPIES OF QUALIFICATIONS– This is essential if you're a school/ college/ university leaver. They aren't

usually required otherwise, but if they are, you'll typically be informed before the interview, and you must remember to take them with you.

7. COPIES/DETAILS OF PROFESSIONAL MEMBERSHIPS – If you are applying for a role that requires you to be part of a professional body, e.g. Human Resources, Accountancy, Law, etc. make sure you take your membership details with you. They are likely to be a condition of employment, and some recruiters like to check them before they'll make an offer. Many recruitment consultants will require them before they'll work with you too.

8. EXAMPLES OF YOUR WORK – Again, I'd advise this if you're a school/ college/ university leaver as you aren't likely to have much relevant experience from which to draw. I'd also suggest this if you're applying for a creative or professional role, e.g. architect, marketing executive, designer, etc. It's likely that a prospective employer would want to see copies of your work as part of the interview.

9. COPIES OF YOUR 'RIGHT TO WORK' DOCUMENTS – This is covered in more detail in book 5 in the Your Dream Job series, 'Managing Job Offers'. Most companies do not require this information until the job offer stage. However, if the interviewer requests that you

bring it to your interview; remember to put it in your folder.

Managing Nerves

The main reason people give for failing interviews is 'excessive nerves', and it's usually top of the agenda for most delegates attending our outplacement programmes. In this section, I'll give you some great tools and techniques for managing your nerves. However, you don't want to remove them entirely as they serve an essential purpose; they help you perform at a higher level. When we are nervous, we produce adrenaline which contributes towards increased performance. The important thing is to manage them so that they don't get out of control, causing an adverse effect.

Top Tips For Managing Nerves

1. Do your preparation – One reason for interview nerves is due to feeling out of control. Most people are under the misapprehension that they don't know what questions they will be asked in an interview, which can lead to experiencing negative emotions. Hopefully, by now, you've realised that it's not true; you *do* know. You will be asked to demonstrate your

achievements, skills, and experience, as well as what you know about the company. Therefore, it's incredibly important to prepare adequately by completing the following activities:

- Write down and practise saying your achievements out loud using the STAR format.

- Prepare your answers for the top frequently asked questions.

- Do your research on the company.

- Know the competencies you will be assessed against (if applicable).

- Write your quality questions for the interviewer.

- Prepare the relevant information to take to the interview with you.

- Practise visualising everything going well.

This amount of preparation covers 80-85% of an interview. I know it seems like a lot of work, however, *'we get out what we put in.'* Clients who follow this advice find that their nerves almost disappear, leaving only a healthy amount. **It takes approximately 3 hours to prepare for an interview adequately.**

2. BREATHE DEEPLY - When we become stressed or anxious, our breathing tends to become shallower. The following is an excellent exercise that you can use to control your breathing, making you instantly feel better. It calms and relaxes the body and mind; the good thing about it is that no-one will know that you're doing it, and it can be done anywhere:

DEEP BREATHING EXERCISE

1. *Take ten* deep breaths:
   - In and out counts as one breath
   - Breathe in through the nose/out through the mouth

2. While breathing deeply, think of something you find calming, e.g. a beautiful beach, walking in the countryside, etc.

3. Repeat as necessary

Once you reach around six/seven breaths, physiological changes occur in the body: feel-good hormones (endorphins) are released that counteract the stress hormone (cortisol) which the body releases when we're feeling stressed.

---

3. VISUALISE THE OUTCOME YOU WANT – I've already talked about the importance of visualisation, it's critical in delivering interview excellence.

4. ACT LIKE A SUPERHERO! - We've all heard the term *'Fake it 'til you make it'* and now there is evidence that supports that it actually works when we change our physiology. We can trick our brains into producing different emotions by purposefully changing our body language to that of the emotion that we want to experience. Even better than that is the fact that not only can we improve our mood, but we can influence hormone release (our biochemistry) by changing our physiology.

Recent research by a lady called Amy Cuddy has confirmed that adopting a 'power stance' (think of a superhero posture, legs spread, hands on hips, elbows bent and chin up) conveys a sense of the individual having power. Furthermore, tests have proven that adopting this stance for two minutes affects our release of the hormones testosterone (increases) and cortisol (decreases). Why these two hormones?

- TESTOSTERONE - Research on testosterone in relation to power indicates that testosterone levels increase when we anticipate competing (it's the same for men and women), as well as after winning, but testosterone levels drop when we lose. In other words, testosterone goes up with the possibility of, or with actual power and decreases when power, or the opportunity to attain power, is lost.

- CORTISOL - Sometimes referred to as a 'stress hormone' because its levels often rise with stress. People who are powerful or hold powerful positions tend to have lower baseline levels of cortisol and, when stressed, their cortisol levels don't rise as much as in people who are relatively powerless or *perceive* that they are.

INCREASE YOUR POWER EXERCISE

Whenever you want to increase your power, e.g. your confidence and self-esteem, etc. do this exercise to trick your mind and body into actually experiencing physiological changes which will supercharge your performance:

1. Stand up tall with your feet apart.

2. Put your hands on your hips.

---

3. Tighten your stomach muscles.

4. Put your shoulders back and push your chest out

5. Lift your chin.

6. Take a deep breath and say, *"I'm magnificent!"*

7. If you can, actually walk around taking large, confident strides (you could even imagine a Superhero cape on your back if you like!).

8. Hold this stance for two minutes, and you'll have no option but to feel more powerful as your physiology will automatically change your biochemistry.

I appreciate that you may feel a little silly doing this, but it does work, and all the research is there to back it up, just Google 'Superman Stance.'

I teach this to clients who would like to feel more confident in challenging conditions such as interviews, presentations or public speaking. I urge them to go to the washroom (if there isn't anywhere else that they can be alone) and stand in a cubical for two minutes doing the 'Superhero Stance.' OK, it may not be the best surroundings, but the results will be the same; you'll feel more confident and positive.

Stand like a superhero, feel like a superhero, act like a superhero!

VISUALISE YOUR DESIRED OUTCOME

I can't stress enough the power that visualisation has on our lives as *'the mind can't tell the difference between something that's vividly imagined and something real'*. The more you practise visualising the outcome you want, the more likely you are to achieve it. The great thing about it is that it's easy to do, you can do it anywhere, and no-one needs to know you're doing it.

When you do something for the first time, whether you do it for real or in your mind's eye, you create a new neural pathway. The more times you practise doing that thing, envisioning it clearly in your mind, the deeper the neural pathway will become and the easier it will be to do in real life.

Visualisation in sport isn't even questioned now. It forms an essential part of all professional sports person's training, and yet it isn't widely used outside of that profession. Why when we know that it works? Visualising the outcome you want significantly increases your chance of getting it.

You can use visualisation for any important event where you may be nervous or if you have to produce an outstanding performance. I suggest that you take some time to clearly visualise the positive outcome you want from your interview/ presentation/ assessment centre.

To visualise effectively you should picture the whole day from beginning to end *going perfectly*. Break down your day into chunks, e.g.:

1. Getting up in the morning.

2. Showering, dressing, breakfast, etc.

3. Leaving the house, getting to the venue early with time to sit calmly and do your visualisation before the interview.

4. The interview/ presentation/ assessment centre itself.

5. After the interview.

6. Going home or to your next meeting.

Visualise everything in as much detail as possible. See what you would see, feel what you would feel and hear what you would hear if it were real. Turn it into a mini video and watch it at least three times a day; morning, noon and night to embed in your subconscious what it is that you want.

It's critical to visualise *everything going perfectly/ achieving everything you want*, because if you imagine anything negative, then that's what you're likely to experience in real life. The more you visualise things going flawlessly, by the time you come to the real thing, your mind already knows what to expect and exactly what you need to do because it's been programmed it into your subconscious.

If you ask any successful person, they will tell you they imagined creating their multi-million selling widget, or they have visualised running a multi-national corporation or "always dreamed" of owning their own business. Everything starts with a thought and imagining how you want your life to be whether you're consciously aware of it or not. ***THOUGHTS BECOME THINGS!***

AFTER THE INTERVIEW

Make a note of what went well and what you think could be improved upon. Do it as soon as you can afterwards so that it's still fresh in your mind. The reason for doing this is so that you can objectively review your development areas and make any necessary adjustments for your next interview whether that's a second interview for the same job or one for a different role.

I realise this exercise can be uncomfortable for some, especially if you're particularly self-critical; however, it's essential for your future performance. Most good companies will provide feedback although it won't be top of their priority list and therefore, you may need to remind them. If you went for the role through a recruitment consultant, they should be able to give you feedback on behalf of their client.

Remember not to take feedback as a negative; although it may feel like it, it's not personal. Take any learning points and incorporate them into your preparation for your next interview/ assessment.

WHAT NEXT?

"If it's important you'll find a way . . . if not, you'll find an excuse."

KEEPING UP MOMENTUM

It's easy to feel motivated in the first couple of weeks of a job search. Looking for the right job is front-loaded as there are more activities at the beginning, e.g. writing your CV, meeting recruitment consultants, joining websites, setting up your profile on LinkedIn and applying for numerous roles, etc. Once all those tasks have been completed, and job hunting turns into more of a maintenance function, it's fairly typical to hit a slump especially if you've received some rejections in the early days.

If you do receive rejections (which is likely), instead of seeing it as a failure, take the learnings and use them to your advantage next time. If you have done every bit of research and preparation that you could have done and still don't get the job, then that job just wasn't for you, and it's likely that there's something better around the corner. Unfortunately, sometimes even though we may think that we are perfect for a job, there can be someone else with more experience, more significant achievements or who is a better 'fit' with that company. We can't change our personality to fit a business, and neither should we.

Through working with so many people, helping them with every type of problem you can think of, one thing I've learnt, without a doubt is that **EVERYTHING HAPPENS FOR A REASON.**

Top Tips - Maintaining Motivation

1. Don't stop applying – One huge mistake that many job hunters make is to stop applying for roles or even turn down interviews when they either have a job offer or an interview invitation. **Never turn down an opportunity until you've received an employment contract and signed on the dotted line**. Until that point, anything can happen. Here are some reasons why you shouldn't stop applying:

- The recruitment process may be paused or stopped altogether by the recruiter; budgets and business priorities are continually changing.

- The offer may be retracted - see Book 5 in the Your Dream Job series, 'Managing Job Offers', for more information on what to do if this happens to you.

- You may be rejected after interview.

Therefore, it's advisable to be prepared by having other things in the pipeline.

I often receive phone calls from clients who say, *"Jo, I've been offered a role, but an interview has come up for another, what should I do?"* My advice is to always go for the other interview. You never know, it could be even more perfect for you than the first.

If you haven't been formally offered a role, it's even more foolish to turn down anything until you've at least explored it. After all, what you're rejecting could be your dream job. I realise that it's more effort (you need to do your research and preparation, etc.). However, it's likely that you'll be in your next position for a few years, so isn't it worth it to make sure it's the right one?

2. BE PREPARED FOR THE LONG-HAUL – Some recruitment processes can take months. At the extreme end, I've witnessed them lasting 6-12 months from advertising to choosing the successful candidate. Often, the more senior the role, the longer the process can take. Don't be disheartened if this happens to you and as I mentioned in No 1 above, don't stop applying for other things. If it's meant to be, it will be!

    If you find that the recruiter is messing you around, e.g. changing interview days/ times, not getting back to you with decisions, adjusting the selection process halfway through, or they don't give you straight answers to your questions, this should be a red flag. In situations like this (and they are common), you need to decide whether this is the type of organisation that you want to work for. If they are like this before you start, what would it be like to work for them?

3. REVIEW YOUR INTERVIEW PERFORMANCE – As soon as possible after an interview, make a note of what went well and any areas for development. Learn from the experience and incorporate that information into your next interview preparation (if necessary).

4. LISTEN TO YOUR GUT FEELING – If something doesn't feel right, it probably isn't; use your intuition. We have an

inbuilt safety mechanism which tells us if a situation/ person/ job is right for us, unfortunately, we often override it. If a job doesn't feel right, if the recruiters don't seem congruent, if you feel like you're being messed around, you probably are.

Recruitment is a two-way process. You have to be happy with the role and company as much as they have to be satisfied with you. If you get a bad feeling about something, either investigate further or leave well alone. Better to walk away from something than end up in a job or company that isn't compatible with you or your values.

5. ASK FOR FEEDBACK – It's perfectly acceptable to ask for feedback after an interview. Recruiters will usually be quite candid about your performance, however, if they are reluctant to try asking, *"If there was one thing I could have done better, what would it have been?"* Again, incorporate any development areas into your preparation for your next interview.

6. DON'T BEAT YOURSELF UP – If you've done everything you can to prepare for an interview and you still don't get the job, it just means that there was someone who had more experience or who was more qualified. Rather than being down on yourself, know that there's nothing else you could have done and be

proud of yourself for preparing so well. Don't let it knock your confidence; that job just wasn't the right one for you. None of your preparation will be wasted, it can be used for your next interview.

7. VISUALISE A POSITIVE OUTCOME – I know that I've mentioned it numerous times throughout this book, but visualisation is an essential tool. You should imagine your perfect outcome in as much detail as possible and run that mini video in your mind as many times as possible during the day.

   If you're going for an interview or presentation, again, visualise it going perfectly. *'The mind can't tell the difference between something real and something vividly imagined.'* Therefore, the more you practise through visualisation, when you come to the real thing, your body will switch to autopilot, and it's likely that you will deliver an excellent performance.

8. BE POSITIVE – Surround yourself with positive people and ignore the doom-mongers. *'We get what we think about'* therefore, it's important to stay optimistic in achieving a positive result. Being around positive people will boost your self-confidence, self-esteem and help you through potentially tough periods.

FREQUENTLY ASKED QUESTIONS

My colleagues and I get asked so many questions during our workshops and one-to-one sessions, many of which are repeated time and time again. Here is a selection of the most frequently asked questions regarding the topics covered in this book:

Q: I've had lots of jobs in different companies, and I'm worried that employers will think that I have no staying power. What can I do about this?

First of all, you need to decide what you really want to do and the type of company you want to work for. The 'Get Clear' exercise described in Book 2 of the Your Dream Job series, 'Finding Your Dream Job', is explicitly designed specifically for this.

If asked at interview why you've had so many jobs, an excellent way to answer is to say that you've tried different things to establish what you really want to do. You've now made a firm decision and are committed to finding and securing a job as an 'X.' However, be prepared to be able to explain the reasons for your choice.

Q: I've had a career gap — I went travelling/took time off to look after my sick relative — how should I explain that during an interview?

Always tell the truth. Many companies view travelling as a positive as it shows that you're adventurous, you can work on your own initiative, you're outgoing and actively seek out new opportunities. As for looking after a relative, no ethical company will have a problem with that as it shows a strength of character, caring nature, and loyalty. If a company does have an issue with you taking a career break, you have to consider whether it's somewhere you wish to work. Is there a possible 'values' clash?

Q: I've been out of work for a while, will that look bad to a prospective employer?

Increasingly people are taking 'time out' after being made redundant. For most, it's the first time in their careers that have the opportunity to take significant time off work legitimately. It's a more palatable way to explain periods of unemployment, rather than saying that you couldn't find a job. Many people decide to go travelling, carry out work on the house, spend time with family, and that's perfectly fine. Most employers no longer have a problem with that, and if they do, again you have to ask yourself if that's the type of company for whom you wish to work.

Q: I've been offered a role but another exciting job has come up, and the recruiter would like me to go for an interview. Should I go?

In short, yes! Until you actually start a job, anything can happen. There is no harm in going along and learning more about the role. After all, it could be your dream job. If you get asked if you have any active applications, don't be afraid to tell them the current state of play. However, be sure to let them know that you are very interested in their role, hence the reason why you didn't turn the interview down.

Q: I've got an interview lined up, and I've been offered another with a different company. Should I go?

Absolutely – presuming it's a role that you're interested in. As I've said before, until you actually start a new job, it's never a done deal. Always keep your options open.

Q: Should I tell the recruiter that I have other interviews in the pipeline?

Yes! There's no reason to lie, and it will indicate to them that you are in demand.

Q: I've got holidays coming up, should I postpone my job hunt until I get back?

No, there's no reason not to start your job hunt. If you are invited for an interview and have a holiday booked within the next six months, make sure you tell the recruiter. I've never heard of a company rejecting an applicant because they have holidays scheduled. If you inform them at the interview, they will usually honour them. Problems start when candidates aren't truthful, preferring to get the role and then tell the recruiter about their holidays. That's dishonest and is likely to get the relationship off on a negative footing.

Q: I've got an interview date. However, I'll be on holiday at that time, what should I do?

Tell the recruiter as soon as possible. Most won't have a problem re-arranging. Alternatively, if timescales are a critical factor, they may agree to a Skype interview. If it's a 'now or never' scenario, it's up to you to decide how important the interview is versus your holiday.

Q: I've just found out that I'm pregnant, should I tell the recruiter?

Technically, due to the Equality Act of 2010, it isn't necessary to tell a recruiter that you're pregnant, and if you do, it's illegal for them to reject you on those grounds. For that reason, many ladies decide not to say anything. However, it's entirely up to you whether you think it's ethical to withhold such information.

Q: All the jobs advertised for my profession seem to be full-time, and I want part-time, should I apply anyway?

This is a difficult one. There are a couple of options in response to this question:

1. Call the recruiter before you apply to see if part-time, job share or compressed hours are an option. The problem with this is that if the hiring company hasn't thought about it before your call, it's likely that they'll say no as it will mean more work for them as they'll potentially need to recruit two people to fulfil the role.

2. Apply anyway and hope for the best. Many applicants do this, turning up for the interview and only when they are offered the job do they say that they want part-time. For some, the gamble pays off because by this point the

company is bought into them and has spent a considerable amount of time and money.

For others, it ends badly with the recruiter believing that there is a fundamental lack of trust in the relationship, and therefore, the offer is often retracted.

In summary, it's up to you to decide what's right and ethical for you in this situation.

Q: I've been in interim roles for the last few years, and now I want a permanent job. Do you think I'll have a problem getting a permanent position?

It's likely that a company will be concerned that you might not stay in a permanent position. You might have to convince them that you want to settle down and that theirs is the right job/ company for you.

There are a number of ways around this depending on your own situation:

- You've enjoyed your time gaining a wealth of experience that you wouldn't have been able to acquire in just one organisation. However, you're now looking to settle down and utilise your skills and knowledge to make a difference in one company.

- You miss working as part of a team.

- You miss seeing the results of your hard work.

- Your personal situation has changed, and you now require more financial security.

Q: Should I reveal my actual salary at the interview?

This is a tricky one. If you are truthful about your current salary, it's unlikely that you'll be offered much more money if you're successful. Companies will tend to go no more than £3,000 higher than your current salary.

I obviously can't recommend that you lie, however, unless you're in the public sector where salaries are very transparent, it's unlikely that they'll be able to find out your exact salary. The only way they can is from your P45, and you don't have to supply that. You can complete a P46 instead, which will ensure that you aren't placed on an emergency tax code.

Q: I got dismissed by my previous company, what should I tell a prospective employer?

As there are so many factors and reasons why people are dismissed, it's difficult for me to give a 'catch-all' answer to this question. Therefore, I would suggest that you speak to a professional career management coach or ACAS for advice on your particular circumstances.

ADDITIONAL RESOURCES

Visit yourdreamjob.co.uk/ and sign up to receive the following documents explicitly designed to complement the content of the 'Your Dream Job' series, straight to your inbox:

- 'Get Clear' Template

- Power Words

- CV Template

- Contact Spreadsheet - Networking

- Contact Spreadsheet – Recruitment Consultants/ Agencies

- Job Application Tracker

- Daily Action Plan

- Covering Letter 1 – Speculative Applications

- Covering Letter 2 – Specific Applications

- Letter of Resignation

You can also join the dedicated Your Dream Job Facebook group:

facebook.com/YDJYourDreamJob/

Your Dream Job Online

Following the success of my corporate career management programmes and the full, 'Land Your Dream Job Now!' book, I have designed the Your Dream Job online programme. It provides step by step instructions and guidance on everything you need to know to find and land Your Dream Job. It is packed full of tried and tested, easy to use tools and techniques gained from working with thousands of job hunters, recruitment consultants, and internal recruiters/assessors, as well as experience from the thousands of new employees I've recruited during my career.

What's Included?

There are three individual courses included in the programme. You can either purchase the programme in its entirety or buy each individual course as needed. For more information on the full programme, visit: https://what-next.teachable.com/p/your-dream-job

Write a Brilliant CV

Write a brilliant CV teaches you how to write a succinct, achievement based, tailored CV using a set template which has been proven to achieve results thousands of times. I will show you what to and what not to include, how to best utilise space and most importantly and how to tailor your CV to a specific vacancy, giving you the best chance of being selected for an interview. For full details of this course visit:

https://what-next.teachable.com/p/your-dream-job-cv/.

FINDING YOUR DREAM JOB

Many job seekers, unfortunately, give up their hunt before finding their dream job, usually because can't seem to find the right role (typically because their search isn't extensive enough), or, they don't get the results they were hoping for and struggle to maintain their enthusiasm. The Finding Your Dream Job course is specifically designed to give you a comprehensive list of vacancy sources and how to get the best out of them, together with how to manage your job hunt so that you maintain your motivation, massively increasing your chances of finding the right job for you. For full details of this course visit:

https://what-next.teachable.com/p/your-dream-job-search/

FOOLPROOF INTERVIEW SKILLS

Most people don't realise, but **YOU CAN PREPARE FOR 85% OF ANY INTERVIEW**, and in this course, you will learn how. Foolproof Interview Skills provides you with everything you need to know to succeed at even the toughest of interviews. It contains comprehensive instructions on how and what to prepare as well as how to answer most general interview questions using a specific, easy to follow formula. In addition, you will learn how to answer the Top Ten Most Asked Interview Questions. I've also included a section focusing solely on what to expect on the day, including how to overcome interview nerves and how to perform at your optimum level, putting you streets ahead of your competitors. For full details of this course visit:

https://what-next.teachable.com/p/your-dream-job-interview-skills/

WHAT NEXT ONLINE TRAINING ACADEMY

To join the 'What Next' online training academy to register for updates on upcoming online training, visit:

https://what-next.teachable.com

Reference Links

For more information on the services that What Next Consultancy (UK) Ltd provides (including one-to-one transformational and career coaching with Jo herself) and to read testimonials about how her coaching has helped her clients visit: whatnextconsultancy.co.uk/

You can also sign up for the What Next Newsletter, a monthly email which includes hints and tips for leading a healthier, more productive and happier life. You can also keep up-to-date with Jo's most recent tips and advice by reading her blog at: whatnextconsultancy.co.uk/blog

Jo also has her own website at: jobanks.net/

Employment Law Advice: ACAS

acas.org.uk/

Helpline 0300 123 1100

Right to Work documentation:

gov.uk/

Job Centre Plus:

direct.gov.uk/en/Employment/Jobseekers/

Citizen's Advice Bureau:

citizensadvice.org.uk/

Recruitment Agencies/Consultancies and Online Job Sites:

- totaljobs.com/
- reed.co.uk/
- indeed.co.uk/
- monster.co.uk/
- kellyservices.co.uk/
- jobsite.co.uk/
- pertemps.co.uk/
- glassdoor.co.uk/
- michaelpage.co.uk/
- hays.co.uk/
- roberthalf.co.uk/
- pertemps.co.uk/
- forrest-recruitment.co.uk/
- manpower.co.uk/
- reed.co.uk/
- bluearrow.co.uk/
- adecco.co.uk/

ABOUT THE AUTHOR

Jo Banks, a Business Owner, Author, Transformational Coach, NLP Master Practitioner, CBT Therapist and author has more than 20 years' experience as a Senior HR Professional, establishing her own Coaching and Consultancy Practice, What Next Consultancy (UK) Ltd in 2009. With knowledge of working within a range of industries, Jo has a strong track record in positively creating high-performance cultures and dealing with complex people issues.

Jo is passionate about helping individuals and organisations to reach their full potential, through her proven and innovative coaching style. While she has trained in the traditional coaching methods, through coaching approximately 1500 people, Jo has found her own unique style focusing on behavioural change and fundamentally changing clients' thought patterns to achieve tangible results, super-charging their performance and elevating their career or business to the next level.

Jo runs inspirational leadership development stand-alone workshops, which include conflict management, communication skills, effective leadership, team development, advanced influencing and communication skills. She has also developed year-long Leadership Programmes which incorporate revolutionary workshops backing up the learning with one-to-one coaching. All Jo's work focuses predominantly on challenging thoughts and perceptions providing a unique blend of information and practical techniques that can put into practice immediately.

As well as providing coaching and leadership development, Jo has developed innovative Outplacement and Redeployment programmes which she and her colleagues deliver to organisations experiencing organisational change. She has combined her knowledge of recruitment (gained from interviewing thousands of people throughout her HR career), plus her insider knowledge of the recruitment industry, with her unique style of coaching to design unique programmes that deliver exceptional results.

Land Your Dream Job Now!' is Jo's second book and describes the very best of her career management techniques. It provides easy to follow guidelines designed to enhance personal effectiveness in putting readers streets ahead of their competitors, enabling them to *'Land Their Dream Job.'*

Jo's first book *'Thoughts Become Things: Change Your Thoughts Change Your World'* is also available at Amazon. It centres on the principles that she uses in her unique style of coaching. It is geared towards changing thoughts and behaviours by providing tools and techniques to understand ourselves and others better, to achieve exceptional results.

Visit Jobanks.net see for yourself the fantastic feedback Jo receives on a consistent basis.

CONNECT WITH JO

Twitter: @JoBanks247

LinkedIn: jo-banks-738b4412

Facebook: jobanks.net/

Instagram: Jobanks247

Web 1:   jobanks.net

Web 2:   yourdreamjob.co.uk

Web 3:   whatnextconsultancy.co.uk

Web 4:   thoughtsbecomethings.co.uk

Blog: yourdreamjob.co.uk/blog

                    jobanks.net/blog

THOUGHTS BECOME THINGS

Change Your Thoughts...
Change Your World

JO BANKS

'Thoughts Become Things: Change Your Thoughts Change Your World' is available now, worldwide from Amazon in both Kindle and paperback versions. For more information visit:

thoughtsbecomethings.co.uk/

Printed in Great Britain
by Amazon

25515734R10128